Matthew Arnold

Higher Schools & Universities in Germany

Matthew Arnold

Higher Schools & Universities in Germany

ISBN/EAN: 9783744771702

Printed in Europe, USA, Canada, Australia, Japan

Cover: Foto ©Paul-Georg Meister /pixelio.de

More available books at **www.hansebooks.com**

HIGHER SCHOOLS AND UNIVERSITIES

IN GERMANY

SECOND EDITION.

HIGHER SCHOOLS & UNIVERSITIES IN GERMANY

BY

MATTHEW ARNOLD, D.C.L.

FORMERLY FOREIGN ASSISTANT COMMISSIONER TO THE SCHOOLS
ENQUIRY COMMISSION

London
MACMILLAN AND CO.
1882

All rights reserved.

"The thing is *not*, to let the schools and universities go on in a drowsy and impotent routine; the thing is, to raise the culture of the nation ever higher and higher by their means."

WILHELM VON HUMBOLDT.

PREFACE.

"IT is expedient for the satisfactory resolution of those educational questions, which are at length beginning seriously to occupy us, both that we should attend to the experience of the Continent, and that we should know precisely what it is which this experience says."

So I said in the preface to the first edition of this work, published in 1868. The history of education on the Continent is now regarded in this country with a great and increasing interest, and I republish, therefore, my account of the schools and universities of Germany. I have abstained from attempting to bring the account down to the present time, either by the addition of chapters at the end, or by the insertion of notes and corrections in the body of the work. A book which, in its original state, was a whole, comes inevitably, by later additions and alterations of this kind, to be a whole no longer. Nor are they requisite for the object of tracing the main lines of the development and character of intermediate and higher education in Germany. These main lines were already there in 1865; they have not come into being between that time and this. It is not probable that they will be changed. There is, indeed, an increasing demand everywhere for modern or *real* studies, as they are called, and the school-course everywhere is being modified in compliance with this demand. But the need of those studies had been recognised by the organisers of German education before there arose a popular cry for them; and now that the popular cry has arisen, it is in Germany that this cry is least likely, perhaps, to be suffered to destroy the true balance of education.

The cost of things has risen greatly in Germany since 1865, and the school-fees mentioned in the following account of German Schools are now, I am told, in many cases the double of what they then were. But the cheapness of good education in the German schools for the middle and upper classes still remains, relatively to its cost with us in England, as noteworthy now as it was then,—as noteworthy for us as the organisation of those schools, and as the universality of their provision.

February 1, 1882.

PREFACE TO THE FIRST EDITION

(1868).

I WAS in 1865 charged by the Schools Enquiry Commissioners with the task of investigating the system of education for the middle and upper classes which prevails in France, Italy, Germany, and Switzerland. In the discharge of this task I was on the Continent nearly seven months, and during that time I visited the four countries named, and made as careful a study as I could of the matters to which the Commissioners had directed my attention.

It is expedient for the satisfactory resolution of those educational questions, which are at length beginning seriously to occupy us, both that we should attend to the experience of the Continent, and that we should know precisely what it is which this experience says. As to compulsory education, denominational education, secular education, the Continental precedents are to be studied; and they are to be studied for the sake of seeing what they really mean, and not merely for the sake of furnishing ourselves with help from them for some thesis which we uphold.

Most English Liberals seem persuaded that our elementary schools should be undenominational, and their teaching secular; and that with a system of public elementary schools it cannot well be otherwise. Let us clearly understand, however, that on the Continent generally, everywhere except in Holland, the public elementary school is denominational,[1] and its teaching religious as well as secular.

Then, again, as to compulsory education. It may be broadly said, that in all the civilised States of Continental Europe education is compulsory except in France and Holland. The opponents of compulsory education quote Mr. Pattison, to show that in North Germany "compulsory attendance is a matter which produces comparatively little practical result." They quote a report of mine, to

[1] Of course with what we should call a conscience clause.

show that in French Switzerland "the making popular education compulsory by law has not added one iota to its prosperity." But yet the example of the Continent proves, and nothing which Mr. Pattison or I have said disproves, that in general, where popular education is most prosperous, there it is also compulsory. The compulsoriness is, in general, found to go along with the prosperity, though it cannot be said to cause it; but the same high value among a people for education which leads to its prospering among them, leads also in general to its being made compulsory. Where the value for it is not ardent enough to make it, as it is in Prussia and Zurich, compulsory, it is not, for the most part, ardent enough to give it the prosperity it has in Prussia and Zurich. After seeing the schools of North Germany and of German Switzerland, I am strongly of this opinion. It is the same thing as in religion. The vitality of a man's religion does not lie in his imposing on himself certain absolute rules as to conduct. But in general, if his religion is vital, it will make him lay on himself absolute rules as to conduct. Above all, it will make a newly-awakened sinner do this; and England, in spite of what patriotic people say, I must take leave to regard, in educational matters, as a newly-awakened sinner.

Therefore I do not think the example of Prussia and Switzerland will serve to show that compulsoriness of education is an insignificant thing; and I believe that if ever our zeal for the cause mounts high enough in England to make our popular education "bear favourable comparison," except in the imagination of popular speakers, with the popular education of Prussia and Switzerland, this same zeal will also make it compulsory.

But the English friends of compulsory education, in their turn, will do well to inform themselves how far on the Continent compulsory education extends, and the conditions under which alone the working classes, if they respect themselves, can submit to its application. In the view of the English friends of compulsory education, the educated and intelligent middle and upper classes amongst us are to confer the boon of compulsory education upon the ignorant lower class, which needs it while they do not. But, on the Continent, instruction is obligatory for lower, middle, and upper class alike. I doubt whether our educated and intelligent classes are at all prepared for this. I have an acquaintance in easy circumstances, of distinguished connexions, living in a fashionable part of London, who, like many other people, deals rather easily with his son's schooling. Sometimes the boy is at school, then for months together he is away from school, and left to run idle at home. He is not in the least an invalid, but it pleases his father and mother to bring him up in this manner. Now I imagine no English friends of compulsory education dream of dealing with such a defaulter as this; and certainly his father, who perhaps is himself a friend of compulsory education for the working classes, would be astounded to find his education of his own son interfered with. But if my worthy acquaintance lived in Switzerland or Germany, he would be dealt with as follows. I speak with the school-law of Canton Neufchâtel immediately under my eyes, but the regulations on this matter are substantially the same in all the states of Germany and of German Switzerland. The Municipal Education Committee of the district where my acquaintance lived would address a summons to him, informing him that a comparison of the school-rolls of their district with the municipal list of children of school-age showed his son not to be at school; and requiring him, in consequence, to appear before the Municipal Committee at a place and time named, and there to satisfy them either that his son did attend some public school, or that, if privately taught, he was taught by duly trained and certificated teachers. On the back of the summons my acquaintance would find printed the penal articles of the school-law sentencing him to a fine if he failed to satisfy the Municipal Committee; and, if he failed to pay the fine, or was found a second time offending, to imprisonment. In some Continental States he would be liable, in case of repeated infraction of the school-law, to be deprived of his parental rights, and to have the care of his son transferred to guardians named by the State. It is indeed terrible to think of the consternation and wrath of our educated and intelligent classes under a discipline like this; and I should not like to be the man to try and impose it on them. But I assure them most emphatically,—and if they study the experience of the Continent they will convince themselves of the truth of what I say,—that only on these conditions of its equal and universal application is any final law of compulsory education possible.

Of the education of the middle and upper classes, however, I have no need to speak at length here, for the following work is devoted to that subject. Secondary and higher education is not, like popular education, a subject which very keenly interests at present our educated and intelligent classes. It is their own education; and with their own education they are, it seems, tolerably well satisfied. Yet I hope that here again these classes,—above all I hope that the great middle class, which has much the widest and the gravest interests concerned in the matter, —will not refuse their attention to the experience afforded by the Continent. Before concluding that they can have nothing to learn from it, let them at any rate know and weigh it.

To three points particularly let me invite their consideration. In the first place, let them consider in its length and breadth the fact that on the Continent the middle class in general may be said to be brought up *on the first plane,* while in England it is brought up *on the second plane.* In the public higher schools of Prussia or France some 65,000 of the youth of the middle and upper classes are brought up; in the public higher schools of England,—even when we reckon as such many institutions which would not be entitled to such a rank on the Continent,—only some 15,000. Has this state of things no bad effect upon us? If the training of our working class, as compared with the working classes elsewhere, inspires apprehension, has the training of their employers, as compared with employers elsewhere, no matter of apprehension for us? There are people who say that the labour questions which embarrass us owe their gravity and danger at least as much to the inadequacy of our middle class for dealing with such questions, as to the inadequacy of our working class. "English employers of labour," these people say, "are just now full of complaints of the ignorance and unreasonableness of the class they employ, and of suggestions, among other things, for its better instruction. It never occurs to them that their own bad instruction has much to do with the matter. Brought up in schools of inferior standing, they have no governing qualities, no aptitude, like that of the aristocratic class, for the ruling of men; brought up with hollow and unsound teaching, they have no science, no aptitude for finding their way out of a difficulty by thought and reason, and creating new relations between themselves and the working class when the old relations fail." I do not say that this is entirely so, but I say that the bearings of our education on the matter,—our education both in itself and in comparison with that of the Continent,—are at least worth studying.

The second point is this. The study of Continental education will show our educated and intelligent classes that many things which they wish for cannot be done as isolated operations, but must, if they are to be done at all, come in as parts of a regularly designed whole. Mr. Grant Duff, who, I must say, directed his attention to educational matters long before they were in everybody's thoughts as at present, has pointed this out with great truth and clearness. Our educated and intelligent classes, in their solicitude for our backward working class, and their alarm for our industrial pre-eminence, are beginning to cry out for technical schools for our artisans. Well-informed and distinguished people seem to think it is only necessary to have special schools of arts and trades, as they have abroad, and then we may take a clever boy from our elementary schools, perfected by the Revised Code, and put him at once into a special school. A study of the best Continental experience will show them that the special school is the crown of a long co-ordered series, designed and graduated by the best heads in the country. A clever boy in a Prussian elementary school, passes first into a *Mittelschule*, or higher elementary school, then into a modern or *real* school of the second class, then into a *real* school of the first class, and finally, after all these, into the special school. A boy who has had this preparation is able to profit by a special school. To send him there straight from the elementary school, is like sending a boy from the fourth form at one of our classical public schools to hear Professor Ritschl lecture on Latin inscriptions.

I come, lastly, to the third point for our remark in Continental education. These foreign Governments which we think so offensively arbitrary, do at least take, when they administer education, the best educational opinion of the country into their counsels, and we do not. This comes partly from our disbelief in government, partly from our belief in machinery. Our disbelief in government makes us slow to organise government perfectly for any matter. Our belief in machinery makes us think that when we have organised a department, however imperfectly, it must prove efficacious and self-acting. The result is that while, on the Continent, through Boards and Councils, the best educational opinion of the country,—by which I mean the opinion of men like Sir James Shuttleworth, Mr. Mill, Dr. Temple, men who have established their right to be at least heard on these topics,—necessarily reaches the Government and influences its action, in this country there are no organised means for its ever reaching our Government at all. The most important questions of educational policy may be settled without such men being even heard. A number of grave matters affecting public instruction in this country, —our system of competitive examinations, our regulation of studies, our whole school-legislation, are at the present moment settled one hardly knows how, certainly without any care for the best counsel attainable being first taken on them. On the Continent it is not so; and the more our Government is likely, in England, to have to intervene in educational matters, the more does the Continental practice, in this particular, invite and require our attention.

In conclusion. There are two chief obstacles, as it seems to me, which oppose themselves to our consulting foreign experience with profit. One is, our notion of the State as an alien intrusive power in the community, not summing up and representing the action of individuals, but thwarting it. This notion is not so strong as it once was, but still it is strong enough to make it opportune to quote some words from a foreign Report before me, which sets this much obscured point in its true light :—

"*Le Gouvernement ne représente pas un intérêt particulier, distinct, puisqu'il est au contraire la plus haute et la plus sincère expression de tous les intérêts généraux du pays.*"

This is undoubtedly what a government ought to be; and, if it is not this, it is the duty of its citizens to try and make it this, not to try and get rid of so powerful and essential an agency as much as possible.

The other obstacle is our high opinion of our own energy and prosperity. This opinion is just; but it is possible to rely on it too long, and to strain our energy and our prosperity too hard. At any rate, our energy and our prosperity will be more fruitful and safer, the more we add intelligence to them. Here, if anywhere, is an occasion for applying the words of the wise man: —"If the iron be blunt, and a man do not whet the edge, then must he put forth more strength; but wisdom is profitable to direct."

CONTENTS.

CHAPTER I.
DEVELOPMENT OF THE GERMAN SECONDARY OR HIGHER SCHOOLS.

The Renascence and the Reformation—The German Schools and the Reformation—Decline of the German Schools and their recovery—The Prussian Schools Representative of those of Germany . . . . Page 1

CHAPTER II.
PRESENT ORGANISATION OF THE SECONDARY OR HIGHER SCHOOLS IN PRUSSIA.

Higher Schools of Prussia—Gymnasien—Progymnasien—Realschulen—Höhere Bürgerschulen—Vorschulen, or Preparatory Schools—Numbers of Teachers and Scholars . 7

CHAPTER III.
GOVERNMENT AND PATRONAGE OF THE PRUSSIAN PUBLIC SCHOOLS.

Common Law of Prussia—State-Action and Regulation—Origin and History of the Central Education Department—Origin and History of the Provincial School Authorities—Provincial School Boards and District School Boards—Examining Commissions—Local and Municipal School Authorities—Endowments and Charities; their Management—Patronage of Schools . . . . Page 20

CHAPTER IV.

PREPONDERANCE OF PUBLIC SCHOOLS. THE ABITURIENTENEXAMEN.

Preference for Public Schools—The Leaving Examination (Abiturientenexamen); its History—Present Plan of the Leaving Examination in Gymnasien—Object Proposed by the Founders of the Leaving Examination—Leaving Examination in Realschulen—Examinations of Passage . . 41

CHAPTER V.

THE PRUSSIAN SCHOOLMASTERS; THEIR TRAINING, EXAMINATION, APPOINTMENT, AND PAYMENT.

Examination for Schoolmasters—Its History—Present Plan of Examination for Schoolmasters — Normal Seminaries for Schoolmasters—Probation and Practising Lessons of Schoolmasters—Appointment of Schoolmasters, and Jurisdiction over them—Intervention of the Education Minister—Religious Instruction—Denominational character of the Prussian Schools—Wide Acceptation of the Denomination Evangelisch—Exclusion from School Posts of certain Dissenters and of Jews — Rank and Title of Schoolmasters — Payment of Schoolmasters 62

CHAPTER VI.

THE PRUSSIAN SYSTEM SEEN IN OPERATION IN PARTICULAR SCHOOLS.

The Berlin Schools—The Friedrich-Wilhelms Gymnasium—Its History—Its Confessional Character, Teachers, and Charges —Its Classes—Its Lessons—School-Books—The Greyfriars Gymnasium—Its History and Endowment—Day Scholars and Boarders in German Schools—The Joachimsthalsche Gymnasium—Schulpforta—The Studientag at Schulpforta —Games and Gymnastics—The Friedrich-Wilhelms Gymnasium at Cologne—Studies of the Gymnasium and of the Realschule—Conflict between their Partisans . Page 98

CHAPTER VII.

SUPERIOR OR UNIVERSITY INSTRUCTION IN PRUSSIA.

Passage from Secondary to Superior Instruction—Special Schools and Universities—Universities of Prussia—Proportion of University Students to Population—German Universities State Establishments—University Authorities—University Teachers—1. Full Professors—2. Assistant Professors—3. Privatdocenten—Students—Fees—Certificates of Attendance at Lectures—Degrees—The Staatsprüfung—Character of the German University System 133

CHAPTER VIII.

GENERAL CONCLUSION. SCHOOL STUDIES.

Probable Issue of the Conflict between Classical and Real Studies —New Conception of the Aim and Office of Instruction—

The Circle of Knowledge takes in both the Humanities and the Study of Nature—This not enough recognised at present—Tyranny of the Humanists—Tyranny of the Realists —Our present School Course—How to Transform it—Excessive Preponderance of Grammatical Studies, and of Latin and Greek Composition—The Ancient Languages to be more Studied as Literature—And the Modern Languages likewise —Summing up of Conclusions . . . . Page 153

CHAPTER IX.

GENERAL CONCLUSION CONTINUED. SCHOOL ESTABLISHMENT.

England and the Continent—Civil Organisation in Modern States—Civil Organisation Transformed not only in France but also in other Continental States—Not in England—A result of this in English Popular Education—English Secondary and Superior Instruction not touched by the State —Inconveniences of this—The Social Inconvenience— The Intellectual Inconvenience—Their Practical Results— Science and Systematic Knowledge more prized on the Continent than in England—Effect of this on our Application of the Sciences, and on our Schools and Education in General—A better Organisation of Secondary and Superior Instruction a Remedy for our Deficiencies—Public and Private Schools—Necessity for Public Schools—With Public Schools, an Education Minister necessary—A High Council of Education desirable—Functions of such a Council—Provincial School Boards requisite—How to make Public Schools—Defects of our University System—Oxford and Cambridge merely *Hauts Lycées*—London University merely a Board of Examiners—Insufficient number of

Students under Superior Instruction in England—Special Schools wanted, and a Reorganised University System, taking Superior Instruction to the Students, and not bringing these Students to Oxford and Cambridge for it—Centres of Superior Instruction to be formed in different parts of England, and Professors to be organised in Faculties—Oxford, Cambridge, and London to remain the only Degree-Granting Bodies—Education Minister should have the Appointment of Professors—Probable Co-operation of existing Bodies with the State in organising this New Superior Instruction—How, when established, it should be employed—Final Conclusion . . . . Page 179

APPENDIX 229

HIGHER SCHOOLS
AND UNIVERSITIES IN GERMANY.

CHAPTER I.

DEVELOPMENT OF THE GERMAN SECONDARY OR HIGHER SCHOOLS.

The Renascence and the Reformation—The German Schools and the Reformation—Decline of the German Schools and their recovery—The Prussian Schools Representative of those of Germany.

THE schools of France and Italy owed little to the great modern movement of the Renascence. In both these countries that movement operated, in both it produced mighty results; but of the official establishments for instruction it did not get hold. In Italy the mediæval routine in those establishments at first opposed a passive resistance to it; presently came the Catholic reaction, and sedulously shut it out from them. In France the

Renascence did not become a power in the State, and the routine of the schools sufficed to exclude the new influence till it took for itself other channels than the schools. But in Germany the Renascence became a power in the State; allied with the Reformation, where the Reformation triumphed in German countries the Renascence triumphed with it, and entered with it into the public schools. Melancthon and Erasmus were not merely enemies and subverters of the dominion of the Church of Rome, they were eminent humanists; and with the great but single exception of Luther, the chief German reformers were all of them distinguished friends of the new classical learning, as well as of Protestantism. The Romish party was in German countries the ignorant party also, the party untouched by the humanities and by culture.

Perhaps one reason why in England our schools have not had the life and growth of the schools of Germany and Holland is to be found in the separation, with us, of the power of the Reformation and the power of the Renascence. With us, too, the Reformation triumphed and got possession of our schools; but our leading reformers were not at the same time, like those of Germany, the nation's leading spirits in intellect and culture. In Germany the best spirits of the nation were then the reformers. In England our best spirits, —Shakspeare, Bacon, Spenser—were men of the Renascence, not men of the Reformation, and our reformers were men of the second order. The Reformation, therefore, getting hold of the schools in England was a very different force, a force far inferior in light, resources, and prospects, to the Reformation getting hold of the schools in Germany.

But in Germany, nevertheless, as Protestant orthodoxy grew petrified like Catholic orthodoxy, and as, in consequence, Protestantism flagged and lost the powerful impulse with which it started, the school flagged also, and in the middle of the last century the classical teaching of Germany, in spite of a few honourable names like Gesner's, Ernesti's, and Heyne's, seems to have lost all the spirit and power of the 16th century humanists, to have been sinking into a mere church appendage, and fast becoming torpid. A theological student, making his livelihood by teaching till he could get appointed to a parish, was the usual schoolmaster. "The schools will never be better," said their great renovator, Friedrich August Wolf, the well-known critic of Homer, "so long as the schoolmasters are theologians by profession. A theological course in a university, with its smattering of classics, is about as good a preparation for a classical master as a course of feudal law would be."[1] Wolf's coming to Halle in 1783, invited by Von Zedlitz, the Minister for Public Worship under Frederick the Great, a sovereign whose civil projects and labours were not less active and remarkable than his military, marks an era from which the classical schools of Germany, reviving the dormant spark planted in them by the Renascence, awoke to a new life, which, since the

[1] See a most interesting article on Wolf in the *North British Review* for June 1865. Not only for its account of Wolf, but for its sketch of the movement in the higher education of Germany at a very critical time, this article well deserves studying; and having been obliged to make myself acquainted with many of the matters which its writer (Mr. Pattison) touches, I may perhaps be allowed, without appearing guilty of presumption, to add that it seems to me as trustworthy as it is interesting.

beginning of this century, has drawn the eyes of all students of intellectual progress upon them.

Prussia was the scene of Wolf's labours, and the Prussian schools, both from their own excellence and from the preponderating importance of Prussia at the present time, are naturally the first in Germany to attract the observer's attention.

As a rule, the secondary schools of Northern and Central Germany are better than those of Southern, and those of Protestant Germany better than those of Catholic. This will hardly be disputed; yet the school system all through Germany is in its main features much the same, and is, in its completeness and carefulness, such as to excite a foreigner's admiration. In Austria this excellent school system is not wanting; what is wanting there is the life, power, and faith in its own operations which animate it in other parts of Germany. Nowhere has it this life and faith more than in Prussia. It has them, indeed, in other and smaller German territories as well; a Prussian will himself readily admit that the schools of Frankfort,[1] or of the kingdom of Würtemberg, are

[1] This was written before Frankfort became Prussian.

as good as his own. But it is in countries of the scale and size of Prussia that a living and powerful school system bears the most noteworthy fruits; and it is in Prussia, therefore, that I now proceed to trace them.

Prussia now, of course, stands for Germany in a degree, even, beyond what could have been anticipated when the above was written.

CHAPTER II.

PRESENT ORGANISATION OF THE SECONDARY OR HIGHER SCHOOLS IN PRUSSIA.

Higher Schools of Prussia—Gymnasien—Progymnasien—Realschulen—Höhere Bürgerschulen—Vorschulen, or Preparatory Schools—Numbers of Teachers and Scholars.

THE schools with which we are concerned, the secondary schools as the French call them, the higher schools (*höhere Schulen*) as the Germans call them, are in Prussia thus classed: Gymnasiums, Progymnasiums, Real Schools, Upper Burgher Schools (*Gymnasien, Progymnasien, Realschulen, höhere Bürgerschulen*). Above these are the universities, below them the primary or elementary schools.[1]

[1] The middle school (*Mittelschule*), variously called *Stadtschule, Bürgerschule, Rectoratschule*, is in truth only an elementary school of a higher grade, and in France is called *école élémentaire supérieure;* in Switzerland, *höhere Volkschule, Secundarschule*.

At the head of these secondary schools, and directly leading to the universities, are the *Gymnasien*. The uniform employment of this term *Gymnasium* to designate them, dates from a government instruction of 1812. Before this they were variously called by the names of Gymnasium, Lyceum, Pædagogium, College, Latin School, and others.

A gymnasium has properly six classes, counted upwards from the sixth, the lowest, to the first (*prima*), the highest. But, in fact, in all large schools the classes have an upper part and a lower part, and each part has, if necessary, two parallel groups (*cœtus*). The sixth and fifth classes form the lower division of the school, the fourth and third the middle division, the second and first the upper division. In former times the *Fachsystem*, or system by which the pupil was in different classes for the different branches of his instruction, was prevalent; since 1820 this system has been gradually superseded by the *Classensystem*, which keeps the pupil in the same class for all his work. The course in each of the three lower classes is of one year, in each of the three higher of two years, making nine in all; it being calculated that a boy should enter the gymnasium when he is nine or ten years old, and leave it for the university when he is eighteen or nineteen.

The *Lehrplan*, or plan of work, is fixed for all *Gymnasien* by ministerial authority, as in France and Italy. It is far, however, from being a series of detailed programmes as in those countries. What it does is to fix the matters of instruction, the number of hours to be allotted to them, the gradual development of them from the bottom of the school to the top. Within the limits of the general organisation of study thus established, great freedom is left to the teacher, and great variety is to be found in practice.

Some years ago the hours of work were 32 in the week. This was found too much, and since 1856, in the lowest class of a gymnasium there are 28 hours of regular school work in the week; in the five higher classes there are 30 hours. The school hours are in the morning from 7 to about 11 in summer, from 8 to about 12 in winter; in the afternoon they are from 2 to 4 all the year round. As in France, there is but one half-holiday in the week, and it is in the middle of the week.

Latin has ten hours a week given to it in all five classes below *prima*, and eight in *prima*. Greek begins in *quarta*, and thenceforward has six hours a week in each class, by which the reader will at once see that we are no longer in France or Italy, but in a country whose schools treat the study of Greek as seriously as the best schools among ourselves. The mother tongue (and here we quit the practice of English schools) has two hours a week in all classes below *prima*, and three in *prima*. But in the two lowest classes it is always taught in connection with Latin and by the same teacher, and time may, if necessary, be taken from Latin to give to it. Arithmetic or mathematics have four hours a week in *secunda* and *prima*, three in *quinta*, *quarta*, and *tertia*, and four again in the lowest class. French begins in *quinta*, and is the only modern language except their own which the boys learn as part of the regular school work; it has three hours a week in *quinta*, and two in all the classes above. Many gymnasiums offer their pupils the opportunity of learning English or Italian, but as an extra matter. Geography and history have two hours a week in *sexta* and *quinta*, and thenceforward three hours. The natural sciences get two hours in *prima* and one in *secunda*; in the rest of the school they are the most movable part of the work, the school authorities having it in their power to take time from them to give to arithmetic, geography, and history, or to add time to them in places where there is no *Realschule* and the boys in the middle of the gymnasium wish to study the natural sciences in preference to Greek. Drawing is a part of the regular school work in the three lower classes of the school, and has two hours a week. *Sexta* and *quinta* have three hours a week of the writing master.

Every class has religious instruction; *sexta* and *quinta* for three hours a week, the four higher classes for two. All the boys learn singing and gymnastics, and all who are destined for the theological faculty at the university learn in *secunda* and *prima* Hebrew; but these three matters do not come into the regular school hours.

I have said that in places where there is no *Realschule*, boys in the middle division of a gymnasium may substitute other studies for that of Greek. Where there is a *Realschule* accessible, this is not permitted; and in the upper division of a gymnasium it is nowhere permitted. In general, the gymnasium is steadily to regard the *allgemeine wissenschaftliche Bildung* of the pupil, the formation of his mind and of his powers of knowledge, without prematurely taking thought for the practical applicability of what he studies. It is expressly forbidden to give this practical or professional turn to the studies of a pupil in the highest forms of a gymnasium, even when he is destined for the army.

Progymnasiums are merely gymnasiums without their higher classes. Most progymnasiums have the lower and middle divisions of a gymnasium, four classes; some have only the lower divisions and half of the middle, three classes; some, again, have all the classes except *prima*. The progymnasium follows, so far as it has the same classes, the *Lehrplan* of the gymnasium. In the small towns, where it is not possible to maintain at once a progymnasium and a *Realschule*, the progymnasium has often parallel classes for classical and for non-classical studies. But, in general, the tendency within the last five years has been for the progymnasium to develop itself into the full gymnasium, and when I was at Berlin Dr. Wiese, a member of the Council of Education there, to whom I am indebted for much valuable assistance,[1] pointed out to me on the map a number of places, scattered all about the Prussian dominions, where this process was either just completed or still going on.

To reform the old methods of teaching the classics, to reduce their preponderance, to make school studies bear more directly upon the wants of practical life, and to aim at imparting what is called "useful knowledge," were projects not unknown to the seventeenth and eighteenth century as well as to ours. Comenius, a Moravian by birth, who in 1641 was invited to England in

[1] Dr. Wiese has written an interesting work on the English public schools; but his book on those of Prussia, *Das höhere Schulwesen in Preussen*, Berlin, 1864 (pp. 740), is a mine of the fullest, most authentic information on the subject of which it treats, and is indispensable for all who have to study this closely.

order to remodel the schools here, and in the following century Rousseau in France and Basedow in Germany, promulgated, with various degrees of notoriety and success, various schemes with one or other of these objects. The Philanthropinum of Dessau, an institution established in pursuance of them, was an experiment which made much noise in its day. It was broken up about 1780, but its impulse and the ideas which set this impulse in motion, continued, and bear fruit in the *Realschulen*. The name *Realschule* was first used at Halle; a school with that title was established there by Christoph Semler, in 1738. This *Realschule* did not last long, but it was followed by others in different parts of the country. They took a long time to hit their right line and to succeed; it is said to be only from 1822 that the first really good specimen dates. This one was at Berlin, and though it did not begin to work thoroughly well till 1822, it had been founded in 1747, and had been in existence ever since that time. Its founder's name was Johann Hecker, who was a Berlin parish clergyman. The Government began to occupy itself with the *Realschulen* in 1832, and as the growth of industry and the spread of the modern spirit gave them more and more importance, a definite plan and course had to be framed for them, as for the *Gymnasien*. This was done in 1859.[1] *Realschulen* were distinguished as of three kinds; *Realschulen* of the first rank, *Realschulen* of the second rank, and higher Burgher Schools. For *Realschulen* of the first rank the number and system of classes was the same as that for the *Gymnasien;* the full course was of nine years. The *Lehrplan* fixes a rather greater number of hours of school work for them than the *Gymnasien* have; 30 for the lowest class, 31 for the class next above, 32 for each of the four others.

All three kinds of *Realschulen* are for boys destined to callings for which university studies are not required. But Latin is still obligatory in *Realschulen* of the first rank, and in the three lower classes of these schools it has more time allotted to it than any other subject. In the

---

[1] By the *Unterrichts- und Prüfungsordnung für die Realschulen und die höheren Bürgerschulen* of the 6th of October in that year.

highest class it comes to its minimum of time, three hours; and in this class, and in *secunda*, the time given to mathematics and the natural sciences amounts altogether to eleven hours a week. As the *Realschule* leads, not to the university, but to business, English becomes obligatory in it as well as French. French, however, has most time allotted to it. Religious instruction has the same number of hours here as in the *Gymnasien*. Drawing, which in the *Gymnasien* ceases after *quarta* to be a part of the regular school work, has in the *Realschule* two hours a week in each of the five classes below *prima*, and three in *prima*.

It is found that after *quarta*, that is after three years of school, many of the *Realschule* boys leave; and an attempt is therefore made to render the first three years' course as substantial and as complete in itself as possible.

The *Realschulen* of the second rank have the six classes of those of the first; but they are distinguished from them by not having Latin made obligatory, by being free to make their course a seven years' course instead of a nine, and, in general, by being allowed a considerable latitude in varying their arrangements to meet special local wants. A *general*, not professional, mental training, is still the aim of the *Realschule* of the first rank, in spite of its not preparing for the university. A lower grade of this training, with an admixture of directly practical and professional aims, satisfies the *Realschule* of the second rank.

Where a gymnasium and a *Realschule* are united in a single establishment, under one direction, the classes *sexta* and *quinta* may be common to both, but above *quinta* the classes must be separate.

The term *Bürgerschule* was long used interchangeably with that of *Realschule*. The regulations of 1859 have assigned the name of higher Burgher School to that third class of *Realschulen*, which has not the complete system of six forms that the *Gymnasien* and the other two kinds of *Realschulen* have. The higher Burgher School stands, therefore, to the *Realschule* in the same relation in which the *Progymnasium* stands to the *Gymnasium*. Some Burgher Schools have as many as five classes, only lacking *prima*. The very name of the *Bürgerschulen* indicates that in the predominance of a local and a municipal character, and in the smaller share given to classics, they follow the line of the *Realschulen* of the second order. Still Latin has three or four hours a week in all the best of these schools. They are, however, the least classical of all the higher schools; but several of them, in small places where there cannot be two schools, have gymnasial classes parallel with the *real* classes just as certain *Gymnasien*, in like circumstances, have *real* classes parallel with their classical classes.

As the elementary schools pursue a course of teaching which is not specially designed as a preparation for the higher schools, it has become a common practice to establish *Vorschulen*, or preparatory schools, as in France, to be appendages of the several higher schools, to receive little boys without the previous examination in reading, writing, arithmetic, grammar, and Scripture history, which the higher school imposes, and to pass them on in their tenth year, duly prepared, into the higher school. These *Vorschulen* have in general two classes.

These are the higher or secondary schools of Prussia. Before the Austrian war the population of Prussia was 18,476,500. The latest complete school returns are those for the year 1863. In 1863, Prussia possessed 255 higher schools, with 3349 teachers in them, and 66,135 scholars. She had 84 *Vorschulen*, or public preparatory schools, with 188 teachers, and 8027 scholars. Of the 255 higher schools, 172 were classical schools, gymnasiums or progymnasiums, with 45,403 scholars; 83 were non-classical schools, belonging to one or other of the three orders of *Realschulen*, with 20,732 scholars.

All these schools have a public character, are subject to State inspection, must bring their accounts to be audited by a public functionary, and can have no masters whose qualifications have not been strictly and publicly tried. We find in the year 1865, I will not say in the public schools of England, but in all the schools which by any straining or indulgence can possibly be made to bear that title, 15,880 scholars. In the public higher schools and preparatory schools of Prussia we find 74,162 scholars.

I will not now press this comparison, but will pass on to show in what way the higher schools of Prussia have a public character.

CHAPTER III.

GOVERNMENT AND PATRONAGE OF THE PRUSSIAN PUBLIC SCHOOLS.

Common Law of Prussia—State-action and Regulation—Origin and History of the Central Educational Department — Origin and History of the Provincial School Authorities—Provincial School Boards and District School Boards — Examining Commissions — Local and Municipal School Authorities—Endowments and Charities; their Management—Patronage of Schools.

THERE is no organic school-law in Prussia like the organic school-law of France, though sketches and projects of such a law have more than once been prepared. But at present the public control of the higher schools is exercised through administrative orders and instructions, like the minutes of our Committee of Council on Education. But the administrative authority has in Prussia a very different basis for its operations from that which it has in England, and a much firmer one. It has for its basis these articles of the *Allgemeine Landrecht*, or common law of Prussia, which was drawn up in writing in Frederick the Great's reign, and promulgated in 1794, in the reign of his successor:—

"Schools and universities are State institutions, having for their object the instruction of youth in useful information and scientific knowledge.

"Such establishments are to be instituted only with the State's previous knowledge and consent.

"All public schools and public establishments of education are under the State's supervision, and must at all times submit themselves to its examinations and inspections.

"Whenever the appointment of teachers is not by virtue of the foundation or of a special privilege vested in certain persons or corporations, it belongs to the State.

"Even where the immediate supervision of such schools and the appointment of their teachers is committed to certain private persons or corporations, new teachers cannot be appointed, and important changes in the constitution and teaching of the school cannot be adopted, without the previous knowledge or consent of the provincial school authorities.

"The teachers in the gymnasiums and other higher schools have the character of State functionaries."

To the same effect the Prussian Deed of Constitution (*Verfassungs-Urkunde*) of 1850 has the following:—

"For the education of the young sufficient provision is to be made by means of public schools.

"Every one is free to impart instruction, and to found and to conduct establishments for instruction, when he has proved to the satisfaction of the proper State authorities that he has the moral, scientific, and technical qualifications requisite.

"All public and private establishments are under the supervision of authorities named by the State."

With these principles to serve as a basis, administrative control can be exercised without much difficulty. These principles, however, may with real truth be said to form part of the common law of Prussia, for they form part of almost every Prussian citizen's notions of what is right and fitting in school concerns. It would be a mistake to suppose that the State in Prussia shows a grasping and centralising spirit in dealing with education; on the contrary, it makes the administration of it as local as it possibly can; but it takes care that education shall not be left to the chapter of accidents.

Up to the middle of the last century, however, the higher schools were so far left to this chapter of accidents, that the State practised little or no interference with the free action of patrons. But it is important to observe that the State was always, in Prussia, an important school patron itself, and exercised its rights of patronage, while in England these rights slipped from its hands. Royal foundations for schools are in Prussia very numerous, and in all Prussian schools of royal foundation the patronage remains vested in the Crown till this day. Schools like Eton and Westminster, like King Edward's School at Birmingham, like the grammar schools of Sherborne, of Bury St. Edmund's, and so many others, would have been in Prussia "Crown patronage schools," with a public, responsible, disinterested authority nominating their masters. So far, therefore, even without any assertion of the right of the State to control private patrons, the higher schools of Prussia have a security which ours have not. The assertion of such a State right, beyond the mere rights of the Crown as a patron, appears in the reign of Friedrich Wilhelm I., and gains definiteness and purpose from that time forth. The *General-Directorium* created by this sovereign, in 1722, was a ministerial body with a department for spiritualities (*Geistliches Departement*) to which the exercise of the Crown rights of control over churches and schools were entrusted. This department was in a few years attached to that of the Minister of Justice, and as such it was held by an able minister, formed in Frederick the Great's school, Von Zedlitz, who in 1787 separated the church and school affairs of the *Geistliches Departement*, and committed the school affairs to a High Board of Schools (*Ober-Schul-*

collegium). In the great movement of reconstruction which between 1806 and 1812 renewed the civil and military organisation of Prussia, the Board of Schools was abolished, and the Education Department was made, in 1808, a section of the Home Office. Wilhelm von Humboldt was placed at its head.[1] Finally, in 1817, this Education section became an independent ministerial department, and its chief took the title of Minister for Spiritualities and Education (*Minister der Geistlichen- und Unterrichtsangelegenheiten*). The first Minister was Freiherr von Altenstein. Medicine having been added to the affairs over which this department has supervision, the Minister's full style now is *Minister der Geistlichen-Unterrichts-und Medicinalangelegenheiten.*

When the Education Department was made a section of the Home Office, Wilhelm von Humboldt had two functionaries with the title of *technische Räthe*, technical counsellors, placed

[1] In June 1810, Wilhelm von Humboldt went as Prussian envoy to Vienna, and the rest of his public life was chiefly passed, as is well known, in the diplomatic service of his country.

with him. These *technische Räthe* have now grown into eight, and they, with the Minister and the under Secretary of State for the department, constitute the central authority for the affairs of education.

But in Prussia it is not the central Minister who has the most direct and important action on the schools, it is the authorities representing the State in the several parts of the country. It is from Wilhelm von Humboldt's accession to office in 1808 that the establishment of a fruitful relation between these two authorities, the schools and the central power, really dates. Before that time, in accordance with the notions which closely connected the School with the Church, the provincial authorities with an action upon the schools were the consistories. These were, indeed, State authorities, for their members are named by the Crown, or head of the State; the head of the State being in Prussia far more practically than in England the head of the Church also, inasmuch as in Prussia the Crown is actually *summus episcopus;* the powers of supervision and discipline vested of old in the bishops, and in England, where we have kept our bishops, still vested in them, having gone, in Protestant Germany, straight to the Crown. The Crown as *summus episcopus* exercises its rights through consistories, and the members of the consistories are in consequence nominees of the State. The consistories therefore supplied a provincial State authority for dealing with schools. But the employment of them for this purpose had two evident administrative inconveniences, to say nothing of other objections to it. In the first place, the consistories were in relation at the centre of Government not with the Education Department but with the High Consistory. In the second place, it is only as a Protestant sovereign that the King of Prussia is head of the Church and represented throughout the country by consistories. As a Catholic sovereign he is not head of the Church, and has in the provinces no consistory or ecclesiastical authority which is also a State authority. But Prussia has nearly seven millions of Catholic subjects. For Catholic schools, therefore, as well as for Protestant, a provincial State authority was required, and this authority the consistory could not supply.

The administration of 1808 established in each of the *Regierungen,* or governmental districts, into which Prussia was divided, a deputation for worship and public instruction (*Deputation für Cultus und öffentlichen Unterricht*). These deputations were in immediate connexion with the Education Department at Berlin; they represented, in the supervision of the schools in the provinces, the State authority, and exercised for the most part the Crown patronage. In 1810 were added three Scientific Deputations (*Wissenschaftliche Deputationen*), one at Berlin, one at Königsberg, one at Breslau, to examine teachers for the secondary schools and to advise the Government on all important matters relating to these. The Berlin deputation had for its members the two *technische Räthe* of the Education Department, Süvern and Nicolovius, and besides these, Ancillon, Friedrich August Wolf, and Schleiermacher. The English reader will observe the sort of persons who in Prussia were chosen for the management, at a critical moment, of the State's relations with education

The higher schools of Prussia feel to this day the benefits of that management. Variations took place in the organisation of the provincial authority, as the different divisions of the Prussian monarchy were constituted afresh, but its general character remained the same, and has remained so till this day. Prussia is now divided into eight provinces,[1] and these eight provinces are again divided into twenty-six governmental districts, or *Regierungen*. There is a Provincial School Board (*Provinzial-Schulcollegium*) in the chief town of each of the eight provinces, and a Governmental District Board in that of each of the twenty-six *Regierungen*. In general, the State's relations with the higher class of secondary schools are exercised through the Provincial Board; its relations with the lower class of them, and with the primary schools, through the District Board. In Berlin, the relations with these also are managed by the Provincial Board. A *Provinzial-Schulcollegium* has for its president the High President of the province; for its director the vice-president of

---

[1] I speak throughout of Prussia as she was before her late war with Austria.

that governmental district which happens to have for its centre the provincial capital. The Board has two or three other members, of whom, in general, one is a Catholic and one is a Protestant; and one is always a man practically conversant with school matters. The District Board has in the provincial capitals the same president and director as the Provincial Board; in the other centres of *Regierungen* it has for its president the President of the *Regierung*, and three or four members selected on the same principle as the members of the Provincial Board.

The provincial State authority, therefore, is, in general, for gymnasiums, the larger progymnasiums, and *Realschulen* of the first rank, the Provincial School Board; for the smaller progymnasiums, *Realschulen* of the second rank, the higher Burgher Schools, and the primary schools of all kinds, the Governmental District Board. Both boards are in continual communication with the Education Minister at Berlin, and every two or three years they have to draw up for him a general report on the school affairs of their province or district.

The Scientific Deputations are now replaced by seven Examination Commissions (*Wissenschaftliche Prüfungscommissionen*).[1] The most important business of these Commissions being to examine teachers for the secondary schools, they have seven members, one for each of the main subjects in which teachers are examined,—philology, history, mathematics, pædagogy, theology, and the natural sciences. These Commissions report to the Minister every year.

Besides the central and provincial administration there is a local or municipal administration for schools that are not Crown patronage schools. Matters of teaching and discipline,—*interna* as they are called,—do not in any public schools, even when their patrons are municipalities or private persons, come within the jurisdiction of the local authority; they are referred to the provincial and district boards. The local authority administers *externa*,—that is, it manages the school

[1] The seats of these seven Commissions are the towns of Berlin, Königsberg, Breslau, Halle, Münster, Bonn, and Greifswald. These towns are also the seats of the Prussian universities.

property, fixes the school fees, gives free admissions to poor scholars, and the like; and it nominates, when the patronage is private or municipal, the teacher; but for his confirmation recourse must be had to the State authority, provincial or central. Thus, if local or municipal patrons chose to appoint a master who had not got his certificate from one of the Examination Commissions, the appointment would be quashed. In most towns the local authority for schools of municipal patronage is the town magistracy, assisted by a *Stadtschulrath;* sometimes the local authority is a *Curatorium* or *Schulcommission*. To take one case as a specimen. The two town gymnasiums at Breslau are under a *Curatorium*, of which the composition is as follows: a member of the magistracy (who must be a lawyer), president; two members chosen by the representative body of the commune, and the rectors of the two gymnasiums. This body draws up the school estimate, of which presently; looks after the administration of the school property, sees that the school premises are kept in order and properly supplied with what they want, represents the town at the leaving examinations, or other public solemnities in which the gymnasiums are concerned, has a consultative voice as to any change in the mode of regulating the free admissions, receives from the rector, when he and the majority of the masters are agreed on a boy's expulsion, notice that a boy has been expelled, with the grounds for it; if the rector and a majority of his *Lehrercollegium* differ as to the propriety of expelling, the *Curatorium* decides. It is not the *Curatorium* that nominates the masters, but the town magistracy, subject to approval by the proper State authority. The teaching and all that relates to it are in each gymnasium under the rector's control, who is responsible on this head to the Provincial Board and not to the *Curatorium*.

In cases where the Crown has had a share in endowing a school, or has made a grant to it, it acquires joint rights of patronage with the local patrons, and for the exercise of these rights it is represented by a commissioner, who is always, as such, a member of the *Curatorium*.

Only a few Prussian schools, such as those of Schulpforta and Rossleben, or the Joachimsthal

School at Berlin, have so large an endowment that it can fully support them. But a very large number have endowments of some sort, or else grants from some school charity or other, such as the *Marienstift* at Stettin for schools in Pomerania, the *Sacksche Stiftung* in Silesia for schools in the principalities of Glogau, Wohlau, and Liegnitz, and many other such foundations. The Provincial or District Boards supervise the *externa*, the property concerns, as well as the *interna*, the teaching concerns, of all schools of Crown patronage; but by the Prussian law, wherever there is an endowment, there is a public right to see that this endowment is properly employed; so that there is a public control for the management of all endowments of private as well as of Crown patronage. The school appoints a man of business (*Rendant, Rechnungsführer*) charged with the financial administration (*Cassenführung*) of the school; the authority in whom the patronage of the school is vested (*Patronatsbehörde*) draws out a school estimate (*Schul-Etat*) every three years, showing in detail the school's income, actual and estimated, for the three years about to commence, and its estimated expenditure. In every government district, or *Regierung*, there is a public functionary, whose business it is to review these estimates, and who addresses to the *Rendant* his remarks and requirements (*Revisionserinnerungen, Revisionsforschungen*), which the *Rendant* has to lay before the *Patronatsbehörde*, whatever this may be, *Curatorium, Schulcommission*, etc., and to which this authority must pay attention. An abusive application of trust funds, or of grants from a charity, is thus checked; all expenses not in the estimate have to be accounted for, and all improper expenses are disallowed. The local patrons can only resist by applying to the administrative authority next above that which has dealt with them (*vorgesetzte Instanz*), and this appeal they will never make when they know they have a bad case.

The State has part in the patronage of more than half of the secondary schools in Prussia; in 72 of them as absolute patron, in 74 of them as part patron. The immense majority of the schools of which it is absolute patron belong to the category of *Gymnasien*, the highest and most expensive class of secondary schools. There were, in 1864,[1] 145 gymnasien in Prussia; of 65 of these the Crown had the exclusive patronage. At the same date there were 28 *Progymnasien,* 49 *Realschulen* of the first rank, 16 of the second, and 21 higher Burgher Schools. Of only seven of these had the Crown the exclusive patronage; of three progymnasiums, two *Realschulen* of the first rank, one of the second, and one higher Burgher School. Under municipal patronage were 26 gymnasiums, 11 progymnasiums, 35 *Realschulen* of the first rank, 10 of the second, and 13 higher Burgher Schools. The municipalities thus show that leaning towards *real* instruction which might be expected from them; of the 49 *Realschulen* of the first rank they have 35. What is most striking to an Englishman is the small number of public schools under patronage neither royal nor municipal, but under the patronage of some church, or corporation, or private person; there are but 12 of them altogether, five *Gymnasien,* two *Progymnasien,* one

---

[1] A year later than the year for which I had complete returns, and for which I gave, as the total of Prussian higher schools open in that year, 255. In 1864 there were 259.

Realschule of the first order, and four higher Burgher Schools. The question therefore as to the rights and interests of private patrons of public schools does not take, so far as the number of their school goes, very important dimensions. The total expenditure on the higher schools and their *Vorschulen* was, in 1864, 2,580,684 thalers (in round figures, about £387,100). Of this sum the scholars' fees contributed 1,193,055 thalers; the State, 526,722 thalers; the municipalities, 401,046 thalers; school property produced 384,224 thalers, and benefactions not under public administration, 75,637 thalers. The State is therefore, after the scholars themselves, the great supporter of the public schools, as well as the principal patron of them.

But the reader will ask, in what sense are the schools with private patrons to be called public schools? They are public schools because they fulfil the requirements, adopt the title and constitution, and follow the *Lehrplan* fixed by public authority for the five classes of public secondary schools, and by so doing obtain the *status* and privilege of such schools. Are there not a great many important establishments, then, the reader may next ask, which do not care to get this status, but prefer to be independent? I answer: No school in Prussia can be *independent*, in the sense of owing no account to any one for the teacher it employs, or the way in which it is conducted; because for every school there is a *verordnete Aufsichtsgewalt*, an ordained authority of supervision. But private persons are no doubt free to open establishments of their own, give them a constitution of their own, and follow a *Lehrplan* of their own. There are ten large private schools in Berlin for the class of boys who go to secondary schools; these private schools, however, have the public schools in view, and take boys whose parents do not like to send them very young to the great public schools, classical or non-classical; but when these boys are ready for the middle divison of the public Gymnasium or *Realschule*, they pass on there. These private schools are merely preparatory schools for the public schools, and accordingly they are organised as pro-gymnasiums and as higher Burgher Schools. They represent no anti-public school feeling, no rival line in education. Two remarkable institutions which did not prepare for the public schools, which gave a complete course of secondary instruction of their own arranging, and which were private schools, *écoles libres*, in the full sense of the term,— the *Plamannsche Anstalt* and the *Cauersche Anstalt*, —existed at Berlin not long ago, but they exist there no longer. Experiments of the same kind are being tried eleswhere. The *Victoria Institut*, at Falkenberg, is a prominent specimen of them ; it is a regular private boarding school, charging 400 thalers (£60) a year, and it professes to give the training either of the gymnasiums or of the *Realschulen*, whichever the pupil prefers. The English generally know more of schools of this kind than of the public schools in Germany, because this kind of private school has a boarding establishment and the public schools have not, and a foreign parent generally looks out for a school with a boarding establishment. For the most part he is no judge at all of schools on their real merits ; he sends his son to a foreign school that he may learn the modern languages, and the boy will learn these at a private school just as much as at a public one. But the Germans themselves undoubtedly prefer their public schools. An attendance in the public secondary schools of 74,000 pupils, in a population of 18,500,000, which is Prussia's population, shows that the Prussians prefer them. And it is the same in other German countries.

CHAPTER IV.

PREPONDERANCE OF PUBLIC SCHOOLS. THE ABITURIENTENEXAMEN.

Preference for Public Schools—The Leaving Examination (Abiturientenexamen) ; its History—Present Plan of the Leaving Examination in Gymnasien—Object Proposed by the Founders of the Leaving Examination—Leaving Examination in Realschulen—Examinations of Passage.

I BELIEVE that the public schools are preferred in Prussia, on their merits. The Prussians are satisfied with them, and are proud of them, and with good reason ; the schools have been intelligently planned to meet their intelligent wants. But the preponderance of the public schools is further secured by the establishment in connexion with them of the "leaving examinations" (*Abiturientenprüfungen, Maturitätsprüfungen, Entlassungsprüfungen, Abgangsprüfungen*), on which depends admission to the universities, to special schools (*Fachschulen*) like the *Gewerbe-Institut* or the *Bauakademie*, and to civil and military service of the State. The learned professions can only be reached through the universities, so the access to these professions depends on the leaving examination. The pupils of private tutors or private schools can present themselves for this examination; but it is held at the public schools, it turns upon the studies of the upper forms of the public schools, and it is conducted in great part by their teachers. A public schoolboy undoubtedly presents himself for it with an advantage; and its object undoubtedly is not the illusory one of an examination-test as in our public service it is employed, but the sound one of ensuring as far as possible that a youth shall pass a certain number of years under the best school-teaching of his country. This really trains him, which the mere application of an examination-test does not; but an examination-test is wisely used in conjunction with this training, to take care that a youth has really profited by it. No nation that did not honestly feel it had made its public secondary schools the best places of training for its middle and upper classes, could institute the leaving examination I am going to describe; but Prussia has a right to feel that she has made hers this, and therefore she had a right to institute this examination. It forms an all-important part of the secondary instruction of that country, and I hope the reader will give me his attention while I describe it.

Before 1788 admission to the Prussian universities was a very easy affair. You went to the dean of the faculty in which you wished to study; you generally brought with you a letter of recommendation from the school you left; the dean asked you a few questions and ascertained that you knew Latin ; then you were matriculated. The *Ober-Schulcollegium*, which was in 1788 the authority at the head of Prussian public instruction, perceiving that from the insufficiency of the entrance examination the universities were cumbered with unprepared and idle students, determined to try and cure this state of things. In December of that year a royal edict was issued to the public schools and universities directing that the public schools should make their boys undergo an examination before they proceeded to the university; and that the universities should make the boys who came up to them from private schools undergo an examination corresponding to that of the public schoolboys. Every one who underwent the examination was to receive a certificate of his ripeness or unripeness for university studies (*Zeugniss der Reife, Zeugniss der Unreife*). The candidates declared to be unripe might still enter the university if their parents chose; but it was hoped that, guided by this test, their parents would keep them at school till they were properly prepared, or else send them into some other line. No plan of examination was prescribed, but the certificate was to record, under the two heads of *languages* and *sciences*, the candidate's proficiency in each of these matters.

The *Allgemeine Landrecht*, promulgated in 1794, after complaints had been rife that the universities had still a number of unprofitable students, and that young men went there merely to escape military service, made yet stricter regulations. It ordered the examination held at the university for boys coming from private schools to be conducted by a Commission; and it forbade the matriculation of any one who did not obtain a certificate of his ripeness.

But the omitting to prescribe a definite plan for the examination, and the entrusting them to two different bodies, the schools and the universities, caused the intentions of the Government to be in great measure frustrated. There was no uniform standard of examination. The schools made the standard high, the universities made it low; and numbers of young men leaving the public schools without undergoing the *Abiturientenexamen* there, waited a little while, and then presented themselves to be examined at the university, where the examination was notoriously much laxer than at the school.

The great epoch of reform for the higher schools of Prussia is Wilhelm von Humboldt's year and a half at the head of the Education Department. The first words of a memorandum of this date on a proposal not to require Greek except of students for orders: "Es ist nicht darum zu thun, dass Schulen und Universitäten in einem trägen und kraftlosen Gewohnheitsgange blieben, sondern darum, dass durch sie die Bildung der Nation auf eine immer höhere Stufe gebracht werde,"[1]—might be taken as a motto for his whole administration of public instruction. It was Wilhelm von Humboldt who took the most important step towards making the *Abiturientenprüfung* what it now is. He was the originator of a uniform plan of examination obligatory on all who examined candidates for entrance to the university. Schleiermacher, who, as I have said, was a member of the Education Council, wished to take away this examination from the universities, and to give it entirely to the schools. This was not done, but the course of examination was strictly defined, and a form of certificate, fully indicating its results, was prescribed. The certificate was of three grades; No. 1 declared its possessor to be thoroughly qualified for the university; No. 2 declared him to be

---

[1] "The thing is *not*, to let the schools and universities go on in a drowsy and impotent routine; the thing is, to raise the culture of the nation ever higher and higher by their means."

partially qualified; No. 3 to be unqualified (*untüchtig*). But this plan of reform, which was brought into operation in 1812, could not produce its due fruits so long as the double examination was maintained. After the peace of 1815 there was a great flow of students to the universities; many of them were very ill prepared; but the universities, with the natural desire to get as many students as possible, eased the examinations to them as much as they could, and admitted the holders of any certificate at all, even of No. 3, to matriculation. At Bonn, in 1822, out of 139 certificates for that year, 122 were of No. 3, declaring the holder unqualified for the University; 16 were of No. 2, declaring him partially qualified; only one was of No. 1, declaring him thoroughly qualified. The Provincial School Boards reported to the minister that the efforts of the schools were frustrated by the laxity of the university commissions, which got more and more candidates. The schools in their turn were inclined to make the first grade of certificate a reward of severe competitive examination, which was by no means what those who instituted it intended. The admission to the universities of young men declared to be unqualified, the two kinds of examining bodies with different views and standards, and the threefold grade of certificate, were found fatal obstacles to the successful working of the reform of 1812.

All three obstacles have been removed. The regulations at present in force date from 1834 and 1856.[1] The leaving examination is now held at the *Gymnasien* only. The threefold grade of certificate is abolished, and the candidate is, as in old times, certified to be *reif* or *unreif*. No one, as a general rule, can without a certificate attend university lectures at all; and no one without a certificate of ripeness can be regularly matriculated in any faculty. The examining body is thus composed: the director of the gymnasium and the professors who teach in *prima*; a representative of the *Schul-Curatorium*, where the gymnasium has a *Curatorium*; the Crown's *Compatronats Commissarius* (joint patronage commissary) where there is one; and a member or delegate of the Provincial School

[1] *Réglement vom 4 Juni* 1834, completed by *Verfügung vom* 12 *Jan.* 1856.

Board. The representative of the Provincial School Board is always president of the examining commission. The *Abiturient*, or leaving boy, must have been two years in *prima*. The examination work is to be of the same pitch as the regular work of this class, though it must not contain passages that have been actually done in school. But neither, on the other hand, must it be such as to require any *specielle Vorstudien*. It embraces the mother tongue, Latin, Greek, and French; mathematics and physics, geography, history, and divinity. An *Abiturient* who is going to enter the theological faculty at the university is examined in Hebrew. The examination is both by writing and *vivâ voce*. The paper work lasts a week,[1] and the candidate who fails in it is not tried *vivâ voce*. The examination papers are prepared by the director and teachers, but several sets have to be in readiness,

[1] Specimens of the subjects set for the German and Latin essay at these examinations are the following. For the German essay :—" How did Athens come to be the centre of the intellectual life of Greece ? "—" From Goethe's *Götz von Berlichingen* draw out a picture of the social state of Germany at the time in which the action of the play is laid." For the Latin essay :— " P. Clodio, cum, ut Ciceronem in exilium ejiceret, in animum induxisset, quæ res fuerint adjumento ?—Hannibal· quibus de causis, quod sibi proposuerat, Italiam subigere, non potuit ?"

and the president of the examining commission, who represents the Provincial School Board and the State, chooses each paper as it is to be given out. He also, at the *vivâ voce* examination, chooses the passages if he likes, and himself puts any question he may think proper. The Provincial School Board have at any time the power to direct that the same examination papers shall be used for all the gymnasiums of the province. Each performance is marked *insufficient, sufficient, good*, or *excellent*, and no other terms, and no qualifications of these, are admitted. A candidate who is fully up to the mark in the mother tongue and in Latin, and considerably above it either in classics or mathematics, is declared *reif*,—passes,—though he may fall below it in other things. If the commission are not unanimous about passing a candidate, they vote; the youngest member voting first and the president last. If the votes are equal the president has a casting vote. But the president may refuse to pass a candidate though the majority have voted for him. In this case, however, the candidate's papers must go to the highest examining authority, the *Wissenschaftliche Prüfungs-*

commission in whose district the province is, for their decision upon them. To this same High Commission all the papers of half the gymnasiums of each province are each half-year referred for their remarks ; their remarks, if they have any to make, are addressed by them to the Provincial School Board, and by the Provincial School Board transmitted to the gymnasiums concerned.

The examination takes place about six weeks before the end of the half. The certificates are given out to the successful candidates at the solemnity[1] which takes place in the *Aula* of a German public school at the end of a half-year, or *Semester*. Each member of the examining commission signs the certificate, which, besides defining the candidate's proficiency in each of the matters of examination, has three additional

[1] At this solemnity a dissertation is read by the director or one of the professors, and every European student knows how much valuable matter has appeared in these dissertations. I have before me the dissertations held in the last year or two at several of the schools I visited. The following are specimens of their subjects :—" De Sallustii dicendi genere commentatio.— Criticarum scriptionum specimen.—Der Prediger Salomo.—Die Erziehung für den Staatsdienst bei den Athenern.—Untersuchungen über die Cissoide (mathematische Abhandlung)."

rubrics for *conduct, diligence,* and *attainments,* which are filled up by the school authorities as he deserves.

The candidate who is considered *unreif,* and not passed, is recommended, according to his examination and his previous school career, either to stay another half-year at school and then try again, or to give up his intention of going to the university. If he still persists in going there at once, he may; but he must carry with him a certificate of his present unfitness (*Zeugniss der Nichtreife*), a certificate with the same rubrics as the other, and signed in the same way. With this certificate, he holds an exceptional, incomplete position at the university : he cannot enter himself in any faculty except that of philosophy, and then he is entered in a special register, and not regularly matriculated. He can, therefore, attend lectures ; but his time does not count for a degree, and he can hold no public benefice or exhibition. He may be examined once more, and only once, going to a gymnasium for that purpose; the three or four years' course required in the faculty which he follows only begins to count from the time when he passes.

The reader will recollect that for the learned professions,—the church, the law, and medicine,—and for the post of teachers in the high schools and universities, it is necessary to have gone regularly through the university course and to have graduated.

Candidates who have not been at a public school, but who wish to enter the university, must apply to the Provincial School Board of their province for leave to attend a certificate examination. They have to bring testimonials, and a *curriculum vitæ* written by themselves in German, and are then directed by the school board to a gymnasium where they may be examined. They have to pay an examination fee of ten thalers. If they fail, the examining commission of the gymnasium is empowered to fix a time within which they may not try again, and they may only try twice. They may, however, if they fail to pass, go up to the university on the same condition as the public schoolboys who fail. These *externi*, as they are called, are not examined along with the *Abiturienten* of the gymnasium, though they are examined by the same examining commission; but the boys who come from private instruction are by the minister's directions to have allowance made for their not being examined by their own teachers, and, so far, to be more leniently treated in the examination than the *Abiturienten*. On the other hand, boys who have been at a gymnasium and who have left in order to prepare themselves with a private tutor, are not entitled to any special indulgence. Indeed a public school boy, who, to evade the rule requiring two years in *prima*, leaves the gymnasium in *secunda*, goes to a private school or private tutor, and offers himself for examination within two years, needs a special permission from the minister in order to be examined. So well do the Prussian authorities know how insufficient an instrument for their object,—that of promoting the national culture and filling the professions with fit men,—is the bare examination test; so averse are they to cram; so clearly do they perceive that what forms a youth, and what he should in all ways be induced to acquire, is the orderly development of his faculties under good and trained teaching.

With this view, all the instructions for the examination are drawn up. It is to tempt candidates to no special preparation and effort, but to be such as "a scholar of fair ability and proper diligence may at the end of his school course come to with a quiet mind, and without a painful preparatory effort tending to relaxation and torpor as soon as the effort is over." The total cultivation (*Gesammtbildung*) of the candidate is the great matter, and this is why the two years of *prima* are prescribed: "that the instruction in this highest class may not degenerate into a preparation for the examination, that the pupil may have the requisite time to come steadily and without overhurrying to the fulness of the measure of his powers and character, that he may be securely and thoroughly formed, instead of being bewildered and oppressed by a mass of information hastily heaped together." All *tumultuarische Vorbereitung* and all stimulation of vanity and emulation is to be discouraged, and the examination, like the school, is to regard *das Wesentliche und Dauernde*—the substantial and enduring.[1] Accordingly, the composition and the passages for translation are great matters in

---

[1] *Perverse studet qui examinibus studet*, was a favourite saying of Wolf's.

German examinations, not those papers of questions by which the examiner is so led to show his want of sense, and the examinee his stores of cram.

That a boy shall have been for a certain number of years under good training is what, in Prussia, the State wants to secure; and it uses the examination test to help it to secure this. We leave his training to take its chance, and we put the examination test to a use for which it is quite inadequate to try and make up for our neglect.

The same course is followed with the *Realschulen* and with the higher Burgher Schools. For entrance to the different branches of the public service, the leaving certificate of the classical school had up to 1832 been required. For certain of these branches it was determined in 1832 to accept henceforth the certificate of the *Realschule* or the higher Burgher School instead of that of the gymnasium. Different departments made their own stipulations; the Minister of Public Works, for instance, stipulated that the certificate of the candidate for the *Bauakademie* (School of Architecture) should be valid only when the candidate's *Realschule* or higher Burgher School had been one of the first class, or with the full number of six classes, and when he had passed two years in each of the two highest classes. I mention a detail of this kind to show the English reader how entirely it is the boy's school and training which the Prussian Government thinks the great matter, and not his examination. Since 1832 the tendency has been to withdraw again from the *Realschule* certificate its validity for the higher posts in the scientific departments of the public service; for these posts, the gymnasial leaving certificate is now again required. But for a very great number of posts in the public service the certificate of the *Realschule* is still valid, and for a still greater number of posts in the pursuits of commerce and industry employers now require it. The Education Department issued in 1859 the rules by which the examination for this certificate is at present governed. They are the same, *mutatis mutandis*, with those for the *Maturitätsprüfung* at the gymnasium. The examining commission is composed in precisely the same way; the examination and the issue of the certificates follow the same course. The subjects are: divinity, the mother tongue and its literature, the translation of easy passages from Latin authors, but, in general, no Latin writing; French and English, in translation, writing, and speaking; ancient history; the history of Germany, England, and France, for the last three centuries; geography; physics and chemistry; pure and applied mathematics; and drawing. Excellence in one subject may counterbalance shortcomings in another, but no candidate can pass who absolutely fails in any. *Externi* who want the certificate are admitted to examination on the same terms, and at the same fee, as in the *Gymnasien*. In *Realschulen* of the second rank the examination is easier than in those of the first, but the certificate has not the same value. The *Abgangsprüfung* and *Abgangszeugniss* of a higher Burgher School, again, are still more easily passed and won, but still less valuable. The *Abgangszeugniss* of a higher Burgher School entitles the holder to enter the *prima* of a first-rate *Realschule;* often a very important opening to a clever boy in a small country place, who for one year can afford to go to a school away from home, but could not have afforded to get all his schooling there.

To the passage from the *tertia* and *secunda* of

the gymnasium or of the *Realschule*, examinations are also attached, for which a certificate, if the boy leaves after passing one of them, is given, declaring his ripeness at that stage. For many subordinate employments in the civil service these certificates are accepted. To be a teacher of drawing in a public school, for instance, a certificate of ripeness for *secunda* of a gymnasium or of a first rank *Realschule* or higher Burgher School is required; this if the candidate has not been at a public school and has to be examined as an *externus*;[1] if he has been at a public school, the certificate of his having passed the examination out of *secunda* at a second rank *Realschule* is sufficient. One important employment of school certificates is to entitle the holder to shorter military service (*Zulassung zum einjährigen freiwilligen Militairdienst*). Young men who volunteer to serve for one year, arming and clothing themselves, the term of military service to be then at an end, must, to be accepted, produce a certificate of a certain value, either from a gymnasium or a *Realschule*.

[1] For the examination of *externi* for this lower kind of certificate, the fee is four thalers.

It shows how many more gymnasium boys there are who go through the full school course than *Realschule* boys, that whereas from the *Gymnasien* in 1863 there were 1765 *Abiturienten* from *prima*, from the *Realschulen* in the same year there were but 214. Adding to the 1765 *Abiturienten* 40 *Externen* who passed at the same time, we have 1805 boys who got the classical certificate of ripeness in 1863. Of this number 1563 went in that year to the Prussian universities. Of the 214 *Abiturienten* from the *Realschulen* (to whom are to be added three *Externen*, making 217), 124 went into the public service, 92 into the pursuits of commerce or industry; one went to prepare for the gymnasial leaving examination, that he might go into a learned profession. Evidently the mass of those who go into business leave the *Realschule* before *prima*, and the majority of those who stay for *prima* stay with the hope of public employment. But the minor certificates accessible to those who leave *secunda* and *tertia* promote an attendance at school longer than that which boys going into business would without the attraction of these certificates be willing to give; and they promote, too, a wholesome return upon the school work done, and a mastering of it as a whole; which tend, the school work having in the first instance been sound and well given, to make culture take a permanent hold upon the future tradesman or farmer. Accordingly, it is common to meet in Germany with people of the tradesman class who even read (in translation, of course) any important or interesting book that comes out in another country, a book like Macaulay's *History of England*, for instance; and how unlike this state of culture is to that of the English tradesman, the English reader himself knows very well.

CHAPTER V.

THE PRUSSIAN SCHOOLMASTERS; THEIR TRAINING, EXAMINATION, APPOINTMENT, AND PAYMENT.

Examination for Schoolmasters—Its History—Present Plan of Examination for Schoolmasters—Normal Seminaries for Schoolmasters—Probation and Practising Lessons of Schoolmasters—Appointment of Schoolmasters, and Jurisdiction over them—Intervention of the Education Minister—Religious Instruction—Denominational character of the Prussian Schools—Wide Acceptation of the Denomination Evangelisch—Exclusion from School Posts of certain Dissenters and of Jews—Rank and Title of Schoolmasters—Payment of Schoolmasters.

To insure that the school work, which so much is done to encourage, shall indeed be sound and well given, it is not in Prussia thought sufficient to test the schoolboy and the candidate for matriculation; the candidate for the office of teacher is tested too. This test is the famous *Staatsprüfung* for schoolmasters (*Prüfung der Candidaten des höheren*

Schulamts), and is the third great educational reform I have enumerated (the *Lehrplan* and the *Maturitätsprüfung* being the other two) which owes its institution to Wilhelm von Humboldt. Before 1810 a certificate of having proved his fitness was not required of a candidate for the post of schoolmaster. Municipal and private school-patrons, in particular, made their nomination with little regard to any test of the kind. There was generally in their school a practice of promoting the teachers by seniority to the higher classes, and this practice had very mischievous results. A project was canvassed for giving to the authorities of public instruction the direct appointment to the more important posts in schools even of municipal or private patronage. This project was abandoned. "But," said Wilhelm von Humboldt, "the one defence we can raise against the misuse of their rights by patrons, is the test of a trial of the intending schoolmaster's qualifications."

This test was established in 1810. An examination and a trial lesson were appointed for all candidates for the office of teacher. It was made illegal for school patrons to nominate as teachers any persons who were not *geprüfte Subjecte*. As time went on, the security thus taken was gradually made stronger. The trial lesson was found to be an inutility, as any one who has heard trial lessons in our primary Normal Schools can readily believe, and a trial year in a school (*Probejahr*) was in 1826 substituted for it. In the following year it was ruled that the *pädagogische Prüfung*, which forms part of the examination of candidates for orders, and which had hitherto been accepted in lieu of the new test, was insufficient; and that persons in orders, as well as others, must go through the special examination for schoolmasters. This regulation gave full development to a policy which had been contained in the reform of 1810, a policy which Wolf had long before done his best to prepare and had declared to be indispensable if the higher schools of Prussia were to be made thoroughly good :—the policy of making the schoolmaster's business a profession by itself, and separating it altogether from theology.

The rules now in force for this examination date in the main from 1831. It is held by the High

Examining Commissions (*Königliche Wissenschaftliche Prüfungscommissionen*) of which I have already described the composition, and which are seven in number. The candidate sends in his school-certificate of fitness for university studies, and his certificate of a three years' attendance at university lectures. With these certificates he forwards to the commission a *curriculum vitæ*, such as used to be required from candidates for many Oxford fellowships. The candidate for the gymnasium writes this in Latin; the candidate for the *Realschule* may write it in French. The certificate given takes the form of a *facultas docendi*, or leave to teach; and this is *bedingte* or *unbedingte*,—conditional or unconditional. The matters for examinations are grouped under four main heads (*Hauptfächer*): first, Greek, Latin, and the mother tongue; secondly, mathematics and the natural sciences; thirdly, history and geography; fourthly, theology and Hebrew. This last *Hauptfach* concerns especially those who are to give the religious instruction in the public schools; if they have been examined for orders before a theological board and have passed well, an oral examination is all

F

the divinity-examination they have to undergo before the Commission. Those who are to give the secular instruction have likewise only an oral examination in divinity, and are not examined in Hebrew; but they must satisfy the Commission as to their acquaintance with Scripture and with the dogmatic and moral tenets of Christianity. Candidates weak in their divinity have this weakness noted in their certificate, and the Provincial School Boards are directed not to appoint any teacher weak in this particular till he has been re-examined and has passed satisfactorily; and the *curriculum vitæ* of every candidate has in the first instance to state what he has done at the university to keep up and increase his knowledge of divinity (*seine Religionswissenschaftlichen Kenntnisse zu erweitern und tiefer zu begründen*). These latter regulations date from within the last twenty years.

The unconditional *facultas docendi* is only given to that candidate who in his *Hauptfach* shows himself fit to teach one of the two highest forms, and sufficiently acquainted with the matters of the other *Hauptfächer* to be useful to his class in them.

The candidate who in one *Hauptfach* is strong enough for any class up to *secunda*, inclusive, but falls altogether below the mark in other sciences, receives a *bedingte* "facultas docendi" for the middle or the lower forms, according as his capacity and the extent of his performance and of his failure seem to merit.

All candidates are required to be able to translate French with ease, and they must know its grammar. All must show some acquaintance with philosophy and pædagogic,[1] candidates for the unconditional *facultas docendi* a very considerable acquaintance; and all must satisfy the examiners that they have some knowledge of the natural sciences.

The candidate for a *Realschule* or a higher Burgher School need not take Greek, but he must pass in Latin. His *Hauptfächer* are : mathematics,

[1] The Germans, as is well known, attach much importance to the science of pædagogic. That science is as yet far from being matured, and much nonsense is talked on the subject of it; still, the total unacquaintance with it, and with all which has been written about it, in which the intending schoolmaster is, in England, suffered to remain, has, I am convinced, injurious effects both on our schoolmasters and on our schools.

natural sciences, history and geography, the mother tongue, modern languages. His examination in all the non-classical matters is even more stringent than that of candidates for the gymnasium, because of his comparative exemption from classics.

The trials *pro loco* and *pro ascensione* are examinations imposed when the nominee to a place has not yet proved his qualifications for that place. For instance, the holder of a conditional *facultas docendi* cannot be appointed to a class in the highest division without being re-examined, and the holder of an unconditional *facultas docendi* cannot teach another matter than the *Hauptfach* in which he has proved his first-class qualification, without being re-examined.

A special *facultas docendi* is given to the foreign teacher of modern languages; but even he, besides the modern language he is to teach, must know as much Latin, history, geography, and philosophy as is required of candidates who are to teach in the middle division of a gymnasium. This provision guards against the employment of subjects so unfit by their training and general attainments to rule a class, as those whom we too often see chosen as teachers of modern languages.

The High Commissioners send yearly to the Provincial School Board of each province a report of these examinations for that province, with the necessary remarks. The candidates for masterships present themselves, with their certificates, to the School Board of the province in which they wish to be employed. In certain exceptional cases candidates may be employed two half-years running without a certificate; but at the end of that time, if they have not passed the examination, they must be dismissed.

Those who at the university have taken, after examination, the degree of doctor, and have published the Latin dissertation required for that degree, are excused from the written part of the schoolmaster's examination. When this examination was first instituted, both Schleiermacher and Wolf, being then members of the Education section, declared themselves strongly against allowing any university title to exempt candidates for the *höhere Schulamt* from going through the special examination. Probably they were right, for the seriousness of the degree examination, and the value of the degree, is not the same in every German university. They were overruled, however; but little or no inconvenience does in fact arise from the allowance, in this case, of an equipollent title; because if a candidate brings the degree of doctor from a university whose degrees are not respected, and if he inspires any suspicion, the patrons who are to nominate him, or the Provincial Board which is to confirm him, invite him to go through the special examination first; and if he refuses, or if he cannot pass, his appointment is not proceeded with.

The *Probejahr*, or year of probation, must, as a general rule, be passed at a gymnasium or a *Realschule*, not at a progymnasium or a higher Burgher School. In this way the schoolmaster of the lower class of secondary schools is a man who has known the working and standards of the higher. The probationer is commonly unpaid, but if he is used in the place of an assistant master, the school which so uses must pay him. The schools are, however, expressly directed not to treat the probationer as a means of relieving an overtasked staff, but to give him an opportunity of learning, in the best way for himself, the practice of his business, and to let him therefore work with several different classes in the course of his year. At the end of his year he receives a certificate from the school authorities as to the efficiency which he shows.

The time passed in a Normal Seminary counts instead of the *Probejahr;* but these seminaries have not in Prussia, any of them, the importance of the *Ecole Normale* in France. There is not the same need of the institution in Germany as in France, and no German professor is obliged to pass through it. The *Ecole Normale* is of much more use in giving its student the thorough possession of what he knows and the power of independent application of it than in teaching him to teach; and these more valuable functions of a Normal School are performed in Germany by the *Gymnasien* and the universities, to an extent to which the *lycées* and faculties in France by no means perform them. Hence in France the need and utility of the *Ecole Normale.* The normal seminaries in Germany are connected with the different universities, and designed, in general, to give the future schoolmaster a more firm and thorough grasp on the matters he studies there. The pædagogical seminaries have not been so important or so fruitful to him as the philological seminaries, where this design has been applied to what has hitherto been the grand matter of his studies,—*Alterthumswissenschaft*, the systematic knowledge of classical antiquity. It was as the head of the philological seminary at Halle that Wolf gave that impulse to the formation of a body of learned and lay schoolmasters of which Germany has ever since felt the good effects. This seminary was opened in 1787, and Wolf was its director for nearly twenty years, till the University of Halle was closed by Napoleon after the battle of Jena, and Wolf went to Berlin to be a member of the Department of Education there. During the latter part of Wolf's time at Halle, he was assisted in the seminary by Immanuel Bekker. There are twelve seminarists, with a small exhibition of 40 thalers (£6) a year each; the exhibition was tenable for two years. No one was admitted to an exhibition who had not already completed his first year's course in the university, but students from any of the faculties might attend the seminary lectures. They attended in great numbers, and for the exhibitions themselves there were at the first examination sixty candidates. The seminary lessons were interpretation lessons and disputation lessons, the former being, as the name implies, the interpretation of a given author; the latter being the discussion, between two or more of the seminarists, either of a thesis set long beforehand and treated by them in written exercises, or of a thesis set by Wolf at the moment and then and there treated orally, in Latin, by his pupils. Wolf's great rule in all these lessons was that rule which all masters in the art of teaching have followed,— to take as little part as possible in the lesson himself; merely to start it, guide it, and sum it up, and to let quite the main part in it be borne by the learners. The more advanced seminarists had some practice in the Latin school of the Orphan House at Halle. The more recent statutes of this philological seminary have set forth in express words, as the object of the institution, the design which Wolf always had in his mind in directing it;—the design to form effective classical masters for the higher schools. Every Prussian university has a philological seminary, or group of exhibitioners much like that which I have described at Halle, not more than twelve in number, with a two years' course following one year's academical study, and *Alterthumswissenschaft* being the object pursued. There are generally two professors specially attached to the seminary, one for Greek, the other for Latin. Besides the ordinary members or seminarists, a good number of extraordinary members, and a yet much larger number of *Auscultanten*, attend the lessons. The staff of the philological seminary at Berlin has this constellation of names, from 1812, when this seminary was founded, to the present time :—Boeckh, Buttmann, Bernhardy, Lachmann, Haupt. The philological seminary of the University of Bonn was founded in 1819, and has had on its staff Professors Nake, Welcker, Ritschl, Otto Jahn. The mouth of the student of *Alterthumswissenschaft* in other countries may indeed water when he reads two such lists as these.

At the University of Bonn there is also a *Naturwissenschaftliches Seminar*, founded in 1825

on the express ground that qualified teachers of
the natural sciences in the secondary schools were
so much wanting. Bonn has, too, a *historisches
Seminar* founded in 1861 for the promotion of
historical studies, and also to provide good history-
teachers for the secondary schools. Dr. Von
Sybel, the well-known historian, is at present one
of its professors. The Universities of Breslau,
Greifswald, Königsberg, have likewise historical
seminaries, serving either by statute or in practice
the same end, of preparing specially qualified
teachers of history for the public schools. Berlin,
Königsberg, and Halle have also seminaries either
for mathematics, or for mathematics and the
natural sciences together; these, too, serve, in
their line of study, the same end as the philological
and historical seminaries serve in theirs. Berlin
has also travelling fellowships of a year's duration,
to enable Germans, who are to teach French in
the public schools, to study the French language
and literature in France itself. Two exhibitions
of £45 a year each are attached to the Royal
French School in Berlin, with the like object of
enabling the future teacher of French to learn

French practically and thoroughly. These are Crown foundations; the Crown, associations, and private individuals are all founders of seminaries. The estimate of none of those which I have named exceeds 1000 thalers (£150) a year. It is astonishing how much is done in Prussia with small supplies of money.

Special pædagogic seminaries (*pädagogische Seminarien*) exist at Berlin, Königsberg, Breslau, Stettin, and Halle. Of these the assigned business with their seminarist is "to introduce him to the practical requirements of the profession of schoolmaster;" but this introduction is still to be carefully accompanied by a continuance of his general intellectual culture. In general, the seminarist here must have passed the examination *pro facultate docendi*, and instead of the *Probejahr* in a school he spends two or three years in the pædagogic seminary. Each seminarist has a certain number of hours' practice (six hours a week at Berlin) in a secondary school; he is present at the conferences, or teachers' meetings, of the school to which he is attached, and he lives with one of its older masters. The Berlin *pädagogische Seminar* was founded in

1787, at first with a single gymnasium (the *Friedrich-Werdersche*) assigned as its practising school; since 1812 all the gymnasiums for Berlin have served in common for this purpose. There are now ten regular exhibitioners; but the exhibitions here are good, and the estimate for the seminary is much larger than that of any other seminary I have named; it is 2390 thalers a year. Dr. Boeckh was in 1865 the director of this seminary as well as of the philological one; and this joint direction well illustrates the close relation at present, in Germany as elsewhere, of the schoolmaster with philology. At Stettin the seminary has only four regular exhibitioners; they have good exhibitions, lasting for two or three years. This seminary is for the benefit in the first instance of the province of Pomerania, and the seminarists have to engage themselves to take, when their exhibition expires, any mastership the Provincial School Board offers them, and to keep it three years.

It is evident from what I have said that these exhibitions do not exist in sufficient number to provide seminary training for anything like the whole of that large body of teachers which the secondary schools of Prussia employ. It is found too that the directors and masters of great schools in large towns, who have a great deal to do and constant claims upon their attention, do not like being saddled with the care of seminarists either at their homes or in their classes. The same difficulties tell against their giving to probationers in their trial year due supervision. But it is the living for a time with an experienced teacher and the making the first start in teaching under his eye, that is found to be so especially valuable for promising novices. It is proposed therefore, instead of founding fresh pædagogic seminaries, to make arrangements for selecting a certain number of good schoolmasters, who will take charge, for payment, of a batch of novices (not more than three) for a two years' probationary course before launching them independently; and a *stipendium*, or exhibition, such as is given in the seminaries, is to be bestowed on those probationers whose circumstances require it. It is hoped in this way to provide a preliminary training of two years for all the most deserving subjects who go into the profession.

At the end of his term of probation the probationer gets his appointment. I have said before that for all appointments to masterships in the secondary schools, the intervention of the State authority is necessary. In schools of Crown patronage the appointment is called *Bestallung*; in schools not of Crown patronage it is called *Vocation*; the State can give *Instalation*, absolute occupation; other patrons can only nominate, and their nominee, if an improper person, is rejected, with reasons assigned, by the State authorities. The Crown, exercising its patronage through the Education Minister, appoints, in all Crown patronage gymnasiums and *Realschulen*, the director. The Provincial Boards, in the minister's name and by commission from him, appoint the upper masters (*Oberlehrer*) in these schools, and the rector in all Crown patronage progymnasiums and higher Burgher Schools. The other masters in Crown patronage schools, the Provincial Board appoints by its own authority. The nomination of a director in schools of municipal or private patronage requires the Crown's assent and the minister's confirmation. The nomination of an

Oberlehrer in such schools requires the minister's assent and the Provincial Board's confirmation. The nomination of other masters in such schools the Provincial Board is empowered to confirm without the assent of the minister. All the directors and masters, whether appointed by the State or only confirmed by it, take an *Amtseid*, or oath of office, by which they swear obedience to the Crown. In schools of Crown patronage, when the minister directs, on special grounds, the appointment, promotion, or transference, of a master, the Provincial Board must comply.

The minister, however, has in Prussia a far less immediate and absolute action upon the secondary schools than the minister has in France. In France the minister can dismiss any functionary of secondary instruction; in Prussia he can reprimand him and stop his salary for a month, but he cannot of his own authority dismiss him. Directors and upper masters are under the jurisdiction of the Court of Discipline for the Civil Service (*Disciplinarhof*) at Berlin; this court is a judicial body, four of its members belonging to the Supreme Court of Berlin; and any complaint requiring the dismissal of a director or upper master must be tried before it. From the sentence of this court there is an appeal to the minister ; but he is bound to appoint, for hearing the appeal, two referees, one of whom must be a member of the Department of Justice; and their decision is final. Complaints of like gravity against other masters (*ordentliche Lehrer*) are tried by the Provincial Board, which, like the Court of Discipline, hears counsel and examines witnesses on oath; from the sentence of the Board there is also an appeal to the minister, who appoints in this case one referee only, but the referee, before deciding the appeal, has to take the opinion of the Court of Discipline. Everywhere in Prussia and in all German countries we shall find a disposition to take security against that immediate and arbitrary action of the executive which we remark in France; and though the Germans give effect in a very different way from ours to this innate disposition of the Teutonic race, yet they give such effect to it as to establish a notable difference, —the more manifest the more one examines the institutions of the two countries,—between the habit and course of administration in Germany and in France.

I cannot but think an Education Minister a necessity for modern States, yet I know that in the employment of such an agency there are inconveniences, and I do not wish to hide any of them from the English reader. I have said that in France political considerations are in my opinion too much suffered to influence the whole working of the system of public education. In Prussia the minister is armed with powers, and issues instructions showing how he interprets those powers, which in England would excite very great jealousy. He tells the provincial authorities that no reproach must attach to the private and public life, any more than to the knowledge or ability, of a candidate for school employment; he tells them that they are to take into consideration the whole previous career, extra professional as well as professional (*das gesammte bisherige amtliche und ausseramtliche Verhalten*), of such a candidate; and that schoolmasters should be men who will train up their scholars in notions of obedience towards the sovereign and the State.

I know the use likely to be made, in England, of the admission that a Prussian Education Minister uses language of this kind; and I will be candid enough to make bad worse by saying that the present minister, Dr. von Mühler,[1] is what we should call in England a strong Tory and a strong Evangelical. It is not, indeed, at all likely that in England, with the forces watching and controlling him here, a minister would use language such as I have quoted; and even if it were, I am not at all sure that to have a minister using such language, though it is language which I cordially dislike, is in itself so much more lamentable and baneful a thing than that anarchy and ignorance in education matters under which we contentedly suffer. However, what I wish now to say is, that in spite of this language, the political influence which has such real effect upon the public education of France, has no effect, or next to none, upon that of Prussia. I do not believe that it has more on that of Prussia than it has on that of this country. I took great pains to inform myself on this head. The last few years before 1865 were

---

[1] He is now (1873) removed.

a time of great political pressure in Prussia; I arrived there when this pressure was at its height, and I conversed mainly with persons opposed, some of them bitterly opposed, to the Government. They all told me that the State administration of the schools and universities was in practice fair and right; that public opinion would not suffer it to be governed by political regards, or by any but literary and scientific regards; and that public opinion would always, in this particular, find strong sympathies among the ministers themselves. I heard of one director to whom Dr. von Mühler had refused confirmation because his politics, which had been very strongly declared, were unacceptable. This director I had the pleasure of seeing; he told me himself, what I heard also from others, that his case was an isolated one; and that it had caused such strong dissatisfaction, not only among the public, but to the school authorities who represent the State in the provinces and consider themselves responsible for the march and efficiency of secondary instruction, that the minister had found himself obliged to appoint him, within a very few months, to a Crown patronage school of greater importance than the municipal school for which he had refused him confirmation. The director added, and this too was confirmed by others, that such an intrusion of political feeling as had prevented his confirmation was in the case of a *Lehrer* or teacher,—either an upper teacher or an ordinary teacher,—absolutely unknown.

The truth is, that when a nation has got the belief in culture which the Prussian nation has got, and when its schools are worthy of this belief, it will not suffer them to be sacrificed to any other interest; and however greatly political considerations may be paramount in other departments of administration, in this they are not. In France neither the national belief in culture nor the schools themselves are sufficiently developed to awaken this enthusiasm; and politics are too strong for the schools, and give them their own bias.

I have spoken several times of the religious instruction as forming part of school work and of examinations. The two legally-established forms of religion in Prussia are the Protestant (*evangelisch*) and the Catholic. All public schools must be either Protestant, Catholic, or mixed

(*Simultananstalten*). But the constitution of a mixed school has not been authoritatively defined, and though the practice has grown up, especially in *Realschulen*, of appointing teachers of the two confessions indifferently, yet these *Simultananstalten* retain the fundamental character of Christian schools, and indeed usually follow the rule either that the director and the majority of the masters shall be Catholic or that they shall be Protestant. In general, the deed of foundation or established custom determines to what confession a school shall belong. The religious instruction and the services follow the confession of the school. The ecclesiastical authorities—the consistories for Protestant schools, the bishops for Catholic schools—must concur with the school authorities in the appointment of those who give the religious instruction in the schools. The consistories and the bishops have likewise the right of inspecting, by themselves or by their delegates, this instruction, and of addressing to the Provincial Boards any remarks they may have to make on it. The *ordinarius*, or class-master, who has general charge of the class, as distinguished from the teachers who give the different parts of the instruction in it, is generally, if possible, the religious instructor. In Protestant schools the religious instructor is usually a layman; in Catholic, an ecclesiastic. The public schools are open to scholars of all creeds; in general, one of the two confessions, evangelical or Catholic, greatly preponderates, and the Catholics, in especial, prefer schools of their own confession. But the State holds the balance quite fairly between them; where the scholars of that confession which is not the established confession of the school are in considerable numbers, a special religious instructor is paid out of the school funds to come and give them this religious instruction at the school. Thus in the gymnasium at Bonn, which is Catholic, I heard a lesson on the Epistle to the Galatians (in the Greek) given to the Protestant boys of one of the higher forms by a young Protestant minister of the town, engaged by the gymnasium for that purpose. When the scholars whose confession is in the minority are very few in number, their parents have to provide by private arrangements of their own for their children's religious instruction.

Prussia had, in 1864, 11,289,655 Protestant inhabitants, 6,901,023 Catholic inhabitants. She had nearly 300,000 inhabitants classed neither as *evangelisch* nor as Catholic, and these were principally Jews. In her public higher schools, out of 66,135 boys, 46,396 were Protestant (*evangelisch*), 14,919 were Catholic. The rest, 4820, were Jews.

The wide acceptation which the denomination *evangelical* takes in the official language of Prussia prevents a host of difficulties which occur with us in England. Under the term *evangelisch* are included Lutherans, Calvinists, and the United Church formed on the basis of what is common to Lutherans and Calvinists; Baptists also, Independents, Wesleyans (for there are Wesleyans in Prussia) are included by it, and in short, all Protestants who are Christians, in the common acceptation of that word. The State, however, in Prussia, not only declares itself Christian (*der Preussische Staat ist ein christlicher*, says the *Unterrichtsverfassung* of 1816), but it expressly disclaims the neutral, colourless, formless Christianity of the Dutch schools and of our British schools (*der*

Religionsunterricht darf durchaus nicht in einen allgemeinen Religionsunterricht hinübergespielt werden). So the Protestant schools as well as the Catholic employ a dogmatic religious teaching. In all schools of the evangelical confession Luther's Catechism is used, and all Protestant boys of whatever denomination learn it. Not the slightest objection is made by their parents to this. It is true that Luther's Catechism is perhaps the very happiest part of Lutheranism, and therefore recommends itself for this common adoption, while our Catechism can hardly be said to be the happiest part of Anglicanism.

The various denominations of Protestant Christians are thus harmoniously united in a common religious teaching. But the State, keeping in view the *christlichen Grundcharakter* of itself and its public schools, refuses to employ any masters who are not either Catholics, or, in the wide sense assigned to the term *evangelisch*, Protestants. Dissenters who are not Christians, and specially the *Lichtfreunde*, as they call themselves (they would with us generally go by the name of Unitarians or Socinians), are thus excluded from the office of public teacher, and so are Jews. In a country where the Jews are so many and so able, this exclusion makes itself felt. A Jew may hold a medical or mathematical professorship in the Prussian universities, but he may not hold a professorship of history or philosophy. France is in all these matters a model of reason and justice, and as much ahead of Germany as she is of England. The religious instruction in her schools is given by ministers of religion, and the State asks no other instructor any questions about his religious persuasion.

Restrictions such as that which I have just described are said to be contrary to the provisions of the Prussian constitution of 1850. The Prussian Parliament has begun to occupy itself with them, and it is probable they will not long be maintained.

A master on his appointment takes the title of *ordentliche Lehrer*, ordinary master (the title of under-master is not used in the Prussian schools), or of *Oberlehrer*, upper-master. The *Oberlehrer* is so either by post or by nomination. The posts conferring the title of *Oberlehrer*, posts in the upper part of the school, can only be held by a teacher whose certificate entitles him to give instruction in one of the two highest classes. *Oberlehrer* by nomination are masters of long standing, who as *ordinarii* or general class-masters have done good service, and have the title of upper-master given to them in acknowledgment of it; but the title so conferred does not enable them to give instruction in any class for which their certificate does not qualify them. The regulations direct that there shall be not more than three *Oberlehrer*, exclusive of the director, for every seven *ordentliche Lehrer*; but in schools with a larger staff of *ordentliche Lehrer* than this, the proportion of *Oberlehrer* to *ordentliche Lehrer* may become much larger. The minister confers the title of professor upon masters distinguished by their attainments and practical success. The directors rank as full professors of the universities, the masters with the title of professor rank as assistant professors of the universities. It should be said that in Germany the title of professor confers on its holder a fixed rank, as a few official titles do here in England. The director is more like one of our head-masters than he is like a French *proviseur*, but he does not, like our head-masters, give the whole of the instruction, or even the whole of the classical instruction, to the head class. Often he is not its *ordinarius*. He, like other masters, cannot give any part of the instruction for which he has not at some time proved his qualification. In general he has some special branch in which he is distinguished, and in this branch he gives lessons in *prima*, and usually in other classes too; governing also, as his name implies, the whole movement of the school, and appearing, much oftener than our head-masters, in every class of it.

Formerly few masterships had fixed incomes assigned to them, but it has more and more become a rule of administration in Prussia to give to all directors and teachers fixed incomes, and to do away with their sharing the school fees. Neither the proceeds of these, nor the proceeds of foundations, are in any case abandoned to the school staff, to do what they like with. On the school estimates which I have described, all salaries appear, and all receipts from endowments or from school fees; the surplus of receipts over salaries and other school expenses is funded, and becomes available for enlarging or improving the school. There are few large endowments; in one or two cases, as at Schulpforta, the endowment is allowed to create for the director and the teachers a position above the average, and at Berlin, where the proceeds of the school fees are very great, the masters of the public schools have also a position above the average; but all this is kept within strict regulation, and is settled, as I have said, by administrative boards of public composition, or under public supervision, and is not left to the disposition of the school staff itself. Schulpforta has a yearly income of more than £8000, but of this sum less than £2000 goes in salaries to the rector and masters. The yearly sum funded, after all the expenses of this noble foundation are paid, is not much smaller than the sum spent in salaries.

By a *Normaletat*, or normal estimate, there is fixed for the staff of State gymnasiums the following scale of payments, which is above rather than below the average scale in *Realschulen*, or in any kind of secondary school not of State patronage. The scale has three classes: the first class is for nine places in Prussia, exclusive of Berlin and Schulpforta, which stand on an exceptional footing of their own; the second class is for thirty-four places; the third class for fifty-eight. Of course the nine places in the first class, being the principal towns in Prussia except the capital, have far more than nine gymnasiums. In all the State gymnasiums of these nine places, the scale of salaries is, for the director, £270 a year; for the masters, according to their post and their length of standing, from £90 a year to £195. In the thirty-four places of the second class, the scale is, for a director, £240 a year; for the masters, from £82 : 10s. to £172 : 10s. In the fifty-eight places of the third, for a director £195; for the masters, from £75 to £150. The salaries thus fixed are meant to represent the whole emoluments of the post; when a house is attached to a post, the rule is that a deduction of 10 per cent shall be made from the salary to balance the gain by the house. In some places there are special endowments for augmenting masters' salaries;

thus the *Streitsche Stiftung* gives £455 a year to augment the masters' salaries at the Greyfriars gymnasium in Berlin; but nowhere probably in Prussia does a school salary reach £350 a year, and the rector of Schulpforta, whose post is perhaps the most desirable school post in the Prussian dominions, has, I understand, about £300 a year, and a house. To hold another employment (*Nebenamt*) along with his school post is not absolutely forbidden to the public teacher; thus Dr. Schopen, the excellent Latin scholar at the head of the Bonn gymnasium, is at the same time professor in the philosophical faculty of the university there; but the *Nebenamt* must not interfere with his school duty, and the supervising authorities take good care that it shall not. So far as it does not interfere with his school duty, the public teacher may give private tuition, and in this manner increase his income; but to give private tuition for fee to the pupils of his own form in the public school, he needs the director's consent. Even when every possible addition to it has been allowed for, the salary of a Prussian schoolmaster will appear to English eyes very low.

The whole scale of incomes in Prussia is, however, much lower than with us, and the habits of the nation are frugal and simple. The rate of schoolmasters' salaries was raised after 1815, and has been raised again since; it is not exceptionally low as compared with the rates of incomes in Germany generally. The rector of Schulpforta with his £300 a year and a house, has in all the country round him—where there is great well-doing and comfort—few people more comfortably off than himself; he can do all he wants to do, and all that anybody about him does, and this is wealth. The schoolmasters of the higher school enjoy, too, great consideration; and consideration in a country not corrupted has a value as well as money. As a class, the Prussian schoolmasters are not, so far as I could find out, fretting or discontented; they seem to give themselves heartily to their work, and to take pride and pleasure in it.

What I have yet to say about Prussian schools, their scholars, and their teachers, may perhaps be best said in connection with two or three of those institutions which I visited. In this manner I shall have an opportunity of rendering, by the help of particular illustrations, general results and statements more interesting to the English reader, and more intelligible to him.

CHAPTER VI.

THE PRUSSIAN SYSTEM SEEN IN OPERATION IN PARTICULAR SCHOOLS.

The Berlin Schools—The Friedrich-Wilhelms Gymnasium—Its History—Its Confessional Character, Teachers, and Charges—Its Classes—Its Lessons—School-Books—The Greyfriars Gymnasium—Its History and Endowment—Day Scholars and Boarders in German Schools—The Joachimsthalsche Gymnasium—Schulpforta—The Studientag at Schulpforta—Games and Gymnastics—The Friedrich-Wilhelms Gymnasium at Cologne—Studies of the Gymnasium and of the Realschule—Conflict between their Partisans.

BERLIN has four royal gymnasiums, one with a *Realschule* annexed; four municipal gymnasiums, one with a *Realschule* annexed; four other municipal *Realschulen*, and one higher Burgher school. All these are full; there were, in 1863, 6874 scholars in them, without counting the children in the *Vorschulen* or preparatory schools which several of them have as appendages; but the supply of higher schools in Berlin is not sufficient for the demand, and the municipality, which was spending in 1863 more than £40,000 a year on the secondary and primary schools of the city, is about to provide several higher schools more. All through Prussia one hears the same thing: the secondary schools are not enough for the increasing numbers whom the widening desire for a good education (*der weiter verbreitete Bildungstrieb*) sends into them. The State increases its grants, and those grants are met by increased exertions on the part of the communes, but still there is not room for the scholars who come in, and the rise which has taken place in the rate of school fee has in no degree stopped them. To obtain the State's consent to the formation of a new school with the name and rights of a public secondary school, a commune must satisfy the State authority both that its municipal schools for the poor will not be pinched for the sake of the new establishment, and also that it can provide resources to carry on the new establishment properly, and in conformity with the requirements of the

Lehrplan. This is being done in all directions. Perhaps the most remarkable of the higher schools at Berlin is the *Friedrich-Wilhelms Gymnasium.* The Greyfriars gymnasium (*Gymnasium zum grauen Kloster*) has about the same number of scholars, but with the *Friedrich-Wilhelms Gymnasium* is connected a *Realschule;* a *Vorschule,* or preparatory school, common to the gymnasium and the *Realschule* both; and a girls' school, called, from the then Crown Princess of Prussia who gave it her name in 1827, the *Elisabetschule.* There were, at the end of 1863, 2200 scholars in the whole institution together; 581 in the Gymnasium, 601 in the *Realschule,* 522 in the preparatory school, and 496 in the girls' school. The gymnasium is remarkable as being the only higher school in Prussia, except the *Realschule* on the Franck foundation at Halle, where the receipts from the scholars cover the expenditure of the school. The annual expenditure for the gymnasium, *Realschule,* preparatory school, and *Elisabetschule* together, is in round figures 65,000 thalers; the receipts from the scholars' fees are in round figures 53,000 thalers. The property of the institution is very small, producing about £400 a year only, so the deficiency is made up by a State grant of about 10,000 thalers; this deficiency, however, arises not in the gymnasium, where the school fees more than cover the expenses, but in the schools allied with it.

The history of this institution is the history of many public schools in Prussia. It owes its origin to the Church, and has then in course of time passed under the superintendence of the State. I have mentioned the establishment by Johann Hecker in 1747 of the first *Realschule* at Berlin. Hecker was preacher at the Trinity Church in the Friedrichsstadt, and he grouped together several small schools in his parish under the name of a *Realschule*. The institution throve from the first; in 1748 it had 808 scholars, and 20 years afterwards it had 1267. It was governed by the curators of the Trinity Church and by inspectors of their appointment; and it was supported, having no endowment except a very trifling house-property, by voluntary contributions and by school-fees. The Latin school, which was one of the grouped schools, grew in importance, and at the fiftieth anniversary of the institution it received the name of *Friedrich-Wilhelms Gymnasium*, and in 1803 was rebuilt, with a grant from the king of nearly £10,000 towards the rebuilding. At the great reforming epoch of 1809 it passed with the other secondary public schools of Berlin under the administration of the Education Department; this change being sanctioned, not only by public opinion but by the governing bodies of the schools themselves, with the view of giving to these great and important metropolitan establishments the benefit of a common and intelligent direction. The *Friedrich-Wilhelms Gymnasium* is now, therefore, both for *interna* and *externa*, under the School Board of the province of Brandenburg, to which, as soon as the School Boards were constituted, the central department transferred its direct charge of the public schools.

The gymnasium is by foundation Protestant, and out of the 600 boys whom I found there, only 20 were Catholics and 15 were Jews. The united schools have a joint director and a joint administration of their affairs. They have altogether 66 teachers, of whom 21 are for the gymnasium. Of these 21, 11 are *Oberlehrer*, and of these 11, 6 or 7 have the title of professor. The director is Dr. Ferdinand Ranke, a brother of the historian; he has been nearly twenty-five years director here, and more than forty years in the profession. He and seven of the upper-masters of the gymnasium are lodged in the school buildings, which are very plain; but in the school-court is one of those relics of the past, so far more common in the German schools, as in ours, than in the French,—the inscription on Hecker's original schoolhouse: *Scholæ Trinitatis ædes in Dei honorem, regis gaudium, civium salutem, juventutis institutioni dicatæ.* There are no boarders; a boarding establishment, which originally formed part of the institution, having been done away with in 1832. The scholars all through the school pay the same fee, 26 thalers a year (£3 : 18s.) In the *Vorschule* the fee is the same; in the *Realschule* it is only two thalers a year lower. In one gymnasium at Berlin the scholars pay four thalers a year more than in the *Friedrich-Wilhelms Gymnasium*; in all the others they pay one thaler less. There is very considerable variety in the rate of school-fees in Prussia, the circumstances of the school and locality being always taken into account in fixing it. The rate in the metropolitan schools is of course a comparatively high one, low as it seems to us. Many schools have a rate rising with the class or division; thus in the gymnasium at Wetzlar the boys in *sexta* and *quinta* pay 16 thalers, those in *quarta* and *tertia* pay 10 thalers, those in *secunda* and in *prima* pay 20 thalers. In some schools the rate is as low as eight or ten thalers for the lower classes, and 14 or 16 thalers for the higher. As an average rate for all the gymnasiums of Prussia, 20 thalers (£3) a year would certainly be rather above the mark than under it. The rates in the *Realschulen* and the higher Burgher schools do not in general range below those of the classical schools. Moderate as these present rates appear to us, they are much higher than they used to be; in the *Friedrich-Wilhelms Gymnasium* the school fee twenty years ago was only 16 thalers in *sexta* and *quinta*, and 20 thalers in the other classes. In many provincial schools it was astonishingly low, as low as 2, $2\frac{1}{2}$, and 3 thalers. In a gymnasium I have already mentioned, the *Magdalenen-*

Gymnasium at Breslau, there was, in 1824, a uniform fee of 8 thalers, and there is now a uniform fee of 24 thalers.

In the *Friedrich-Wilhelms Gymnasium* I found that 10 per cent of the 600 scholars had free schooling. The number of free posts, as they are called (*Freistellen*), varies in different schools; in some it goes up to 25 per cent, but I think 10 per cent may be taken as a fair average. These free posts are given on the ground of need and public claim. There are also a few exhibitions in the *Friedrich-Wilhelms Gymnasium;* but it will be best to notice the subject of exhibitions when I am speaking of some older and richer establishment.

Of course in the very large schools it is not possible to actually group and teach the scholars in six classes, nor yet is it always possible to observe the rule which enjoins that there shall not be more than forty scholars in either *secunda* or *prima*, or more than fifty in any of the other classes. The supply of class-rooms falls short, even more than the supply of teachers. The highest class, however, always remains *prima*, as in our great schools it always remains the *sixth ;* and in the higher classes the Germans, as I have already mentioned, follow, when it is necessary, the plan of having an upper and lower division (*oberprima unterprima*), and in other classes both this plan and the plan of having two groups or assemblages (*cœtus*) at the same stage of school work, and advancing parallel to one another.

The first lesson I heard was Dr. Ranke's own lesson to *prima*, on the *Philoctetes* of Sophocles. He spoke Latin to his class and his class spoke Latin in answer; this is still a common practice in the German schools, though not so common as formerly. The German boys have certainly acquired through this practice a surprising command of Latin; Dr. Schopen's lesson at Bonn to his *prima* in extemporaneous translation into Latin, —a lesson which has a deserved celebrity,—I heard with astonishment; a much wider command of the Latin vocabulary than our boys have, and a more ready management of the language, the Germans certainly succeed in acquiring. On the other hand, the best style of the best authors is not, to my mind, so well caught in Latin composition by their boys as by ours. This is more particularly the case in verse, where their best scholars often show, I cannot but think, not only a want of practical skill (that of course is nothing), but a want of tact for judging what is uncouth and inadmissible, which one would not have expected of people who know the Latin models so well. The same is true, in a less degree, of their prose; the best scholars in the best schools of England or France, if set to write a speech or a character in the style of Cicero or Tacitus, would, I think, in general acquit themselves of the task more happily than the corresponding boys of a German school.

But the feeling which was strongest with me in the Berlin *Philoctetes* lesson was the feeling that one seemed to be back in the sixth form at Rugby again, as I remember it nearly thirty years ago. After the lecture rooms at Oxford, and the French *lycées*, and the Italian *licei*, here was at last a body of pupils once more who had worked at their lessons, had learnt Greek, and were at home in a Greek play. What the Berlin boys knew about the scope of the play, its chief personages, and the governing idea and character of each, was more than the Rugby boys would have known; but the quantity of lines done, the style of doing them, and the extent of scholarship expected in the boys and found in them, seemed to me as nearly as possible the same thing at Berlin and at Rugby. I thought the same in the afternoon when I heard Professor Zumpt (a son of the famous Latin scholar) take *unterprima* in Cicero's speech *Pro Sex. Roscio Amerino*. The boys had been through the oration during the early part of the half-year; they were now going very rapidly through it again, translating into fluent German without taking the Latin words. The master let the boys be the performers, and spoke as little as possible himself, but every good or bad performance was noticed. Just the same with lessons in Thucydides, Livy, and Horace, which I heard at other gymnasiums in Berlin. The lessons had been well prepared by the pupils, the master made few comments, and only on really noteworthy matters, or to cite some parallel passage which was not likely to have come within his pupils' reading; in general, when he spoke it was to question, and he questioned closely. I was struck with the exact knowledge of the Horatian metres which the *unterprima* boys at Greyfriars showed when questioned on them. I found that the practice was to begin by taking eleven odes as specimens of metre, and carefully studying these before proceeding further. Then they commence the *Odes* at the beginning and go right through them. The portion of a Latin or Greek author got through at a lesson is about the same as in the corresponding form in one of the best English schools, but either in school or by private study the boys have certainly read more than our boys or the French; it is the general rule that a boy who goes in for the leaving examination has read Homer all through. A large number of the boys, too, seem to have really benefited by the instruction, and to be in the first flight of their class, than with us. But the great superiority of the Germans, and where they show how much further they have gone in *Alterthumswissenschaft* than we have, is in their far broader notion of treating, even in their schools, the ancient authors as *literature*, and conceiving the place and significance of an author in his country's literature, and in that of the world. In this way the student's interest in Greek and Latin becomes much more vital, and the hold of these languages upon him is much more likely to be permanent. This is to be set against the superior finish and elegance of the best of our boys in Latin and Greek composition; above all, in Latin and Greek verse. Greek verse, indeed, can scarcely be said to be a school exercise at all, so far as I could see or hear, in the foreign schools.

Instead of having to write Greek iambics, the boys in *prima* at the *Friedrich-Wilhelms Gymnasium*, on one of the days when I was there, had had to write a summary of Lessing's essay on the epigram. The summaries were handed to the professor, who then made a boy stand up and give in his own words the substance of Lessing's essay, beginning at the beginning, the professor commenting and asking questions as the boy proceeded. Presently another boy was set on, and in this way they went through the essay. The lesson was as much out of the range of my English school experience as the lessons on the *Femmes Savantes* of Molière, which I heard, as I have already said, with so much interest in the *Ecole Normale* at Paris.

The Berlin lesson, like the Paris one, was very interesting.

In the lower division of *tertia* (about the middle of the school) I had another opportunity of observing a way, not, I think, in use in England, of practising the boys in Latin. The lesson was Ovid; the boys had had to translate at home a certain portion of Ovid into German, and then to bring their translation with them to school. This they had then, in school, to turn back into Latin, not metrical. After this, boys were called upon one after another, as in England, to say a few lines of Ovid by heart; but then, again, each boy had also to say in German prose the passage he had just recited in Ovid's verse.

In *quinta* I heard the religious instruction. For boys still so near the primary school stage, religious instruction, as a part of the school lessons, seems to me to be still, as in the primary school, in place, and still useful; in the higher classes of the secondary school, it seems to me, I confess, unprofitable and inappropriate. Anything more futile and useless than the lesson in the *Galatians* which I heard given to *secunda* at

Bonn cannot possibly be imagined. In *quinta* here at Berlin, it was different; the boys were first questioned in Bible narratives from a text-book; a good text-book and good questioning; then they said Luther's Short Catechism, and then they repeated hymns. The two or three Catholic and Jewish boys belonging to the class did not come to this lesson.

The mention of a text-book reminds me to say a word about the rule in the Prussian public schools for school-books. The masters choose the books, but the approval of the Provincial Board must be obtained for their choice; before approving for the first time any new book, the Provincial Board must refer to the Education Minister and his Council. When a book has once been approved for a gymnasium, it may be used in any other gymnasium or progymnasium of the same province; but approval for a gymnasium does not count for a *Realschule*, and *vice versâ*.

I must in passing observe how greatly some intelligent censorship like that of the Provincial Boards and the Minister in Prussia, or that of the Council of Public Instruction in France, is needed for school-books in England. Many as are the absurdities of our state of school anarchy, perhaps none of them is more crying than the book-pest which prevails under it. Every school chooses at its own discretion; many schools make a trade of book-dealing, and therefore it is for their interest to have books which are not used elsewhere, and which the pupil will not bring with him from his last school; so that a boy who has been at three or four English schools has often had to buy a complete new set of school-books for each. The extravagance of this is bad enough; but then, besides, as there exists no intelligent control or selection of them, half at least of our school-books are rubbish, and to the other defects of our school system we may add this, that in no other secondary schools in Europe do the pupils spend so much of their time in learning such utter nonsense as they do in ours.

I have mentioned the Greyfriars gymnasium, where I also heard lessons, and where they were of the same character as at the *Friedrich-Wilhelms Gymnasium*, a character much more like that of the lessons in our best English public schools than of the lessons in the French *lycées*. The history of Greyfriars is this. It occupies the site of a Franciscan convent abolished at the Reformation; in 1574 the third part of the convent premises was assigned by the elector, at the instance of the town magistracy, for use as a public school. The magistracy endowed it, and the elector made it over to them, but with an electoral *Schulordnung*. Here from the earliest times of the school there was a *convictorium* (the Italian *convitto*). The robust appetite of the sixteenth century for the humanities appears in the original plan of work; Greek had thirteen hours a week, Latin ten, logic two, arithmetic two, singing five. In 1655 the school had 400 scholars. In the second quarter of the eighteenth century the mother-tongue and its literature first appear as part of the school course; the German public schools having thus the start of ours, in this particular, by about 125 years. In 1793 the school got the benefit of a great endowment which I have already mentioned, the *Streitsche Stiftung;* the capital of this endowment is now £33,000. It is administered by a *Directorium* composed, not of Sigismund Streit's descendants, but as follows: the provost of St. Nicholas (parish minister), the director and the pro-rector of the school, a councillor of the Education Department, a merchant or tradesman, and a lawyer. The financial administration of this *Directorium* is controlled, in the manner I have already described, by the public finance officers of the *Regierung* or governmental district in which Berlin stands.

Streit's endowment maintains at Greyfriars teachers of the modern languages, of astronomy, and of music, provides a *Wohncommunitat* (lodging, bedding, fire, and lights) for twelve scholars, and a *Freitisch* (board) for twenty-four more; and keeps improving the school library (now 20,000 volumes), the observatory, collections, etc. It also augments the salaries of the director and a number of the masters. Other benefactions provide the widows of masters who die in office with a sum for their husbands' funeral expenses, and a pension of £45 a year. There is an endowment of nearly £450 a year for exhibitions to be enjoyed at the school, and of £150 a year for exhibitions at the universities. Every two years is held a school-festival in honour of founders and benefactors. The school premises had an important enlargement by Crown grants of land in 1819 and 1831, and great additions have since that time been made to the buildings. I found about 550 boys, with a director and twenty-five masters. On an average, twenty-five boys pass the *Abiturientenexamen* from this school every year. Here, too, as at the *Friedrich-Wilhelms Gymnasium*, the number of free posts is 10 per cent. They are provided by the municipality. The school gets a grant of about £100 a year from the State and £1000 a year from the city of Berlin.

By original foundation and by endowment this school too is Protestant. Hardly any Catholic boys are here, but of Jewish boys there are seventy or eighty. About a third of the whole number of the scholars are *Auswärtige;* boys who came from a 'distance, and cannot, therefore, live with their parents. The great *internats* of the French *lycées* are unknown in Germany; the *Alumnate* or *Convicte* of the German schools are properly establishments like *college* at Eton or

Winchester, and are for foundationers; for establishments like the School House and the masters' boarding-houses at Rugby, or Commoners at Winchester, the strict designation would in Germany be *Pensionat, Pensionsanstalt*, and not *Alumnat*. The practice of having one's son live at home and go to school for his lessons only, obtains much more widely in Germany than with us; 40,000 of the 66,000 boys in the Prussian higher schools are day scholars. Still this leaves 26,000 who are not; and of these the vast majority live with some respectable family in the place where they go to school. The household with which their son is to board or lodge is designated by the parent, but must, by the school regulations of Prussia, be approved by the director of the boy's school, who holds the householder responsible for the boy's conduct out of school. The family life in North Germany is in general decent, kindly, and God-fearing; and a boy is, I think, much better placed as a boarder in this way than as an *interne* of a French *lycée*. Still the school authorities in Prussia are of opinion that the provision of boarding establishments in immediate connection with the public schools needs increasing, and they design to increase it.

The patron at Greyfriars, for matters that do not come within the province of the *Directorium* of Streit's charity, is still, as the elector John George originally appointed, the city of Berlin, the municipality. The reader will remember that for the *interna* of a Prussian gymnasium the intervention of a Provincial Board always subsists.

I must give a word in passing to the great *Alumnat* of Berlin, the *Joachimsthalsche Gymnasium*. Here I found 404 scholars; 120 of them were collegers (*Alumnen*), 12 were boarders in the establishment (*Pensionaire*); the rest were the boys who came for the lessons only (*Hospiten*). Ten per cent of these have free schooling. The *Pensionaire* pay only £24 a year; the *Alumnen* are not all of them free of all cost; 25 of them pay £8 : 14s. a year; 75 of them pay £4 : 10s. There are 20 places with board, lodging, and instruction all entirely free, for 20 proved scholars of the highest forms.

The *Joachimsthalsche Gymnasium* is a royal foundation, endowed with lands by the elector

Joachim Frederick in 1607. It is Protestant. The school has now an income of over £3000 a year from land, and of over £2000 a year from money in the funds. The Crown is the patron; the property is administered, owing to its connection with the Crown domain, by the *Regierung* at Potsdam.

This is an interesting school, for the list of its masters contains the names of Buttmann, Schneider, Passow, Zumpt, Krüger, and Bergk. The director is Dr. Kiessling, a son of the editor of Theocritus. Constantly in the rolls of the German schools one is coming upon a well-known name of this kind; on the roll of former teachers at Greyfriars are to be found the names of Heindorf, Spalding, Droysen. Nor are other recollections, as interesting as any school in the world can boast, wanting to the Prussian schools. The Joachimsthal School had a scholar of *quarta* who, like so many German schoolboys, joined the army in the great uprising against the French in 1813. This boy was wounded at Leipzig, made the campaign of France, was at Waterloo, received the decoration of the Iron Cross, and, finally, with the decoration on his breast, took his place again on his old schoolbench as a scholar of *quarta*.

But no *Alumnat* in Prussia, or indeed in Germany, can compare with Schulpforta, which by its antiquity, its beauty, its wealth, its celebrity, is entitled to vie with the most renowned English schools. The Cistercian abbey of St. Mary's, Pforta, dates from 1137. It was secularised in 1540; and Duke Maurice of Saxony, in 1543, established in its place and endowed with its revenues a Protestant school for 100 scholars. It stands near the Saal, in the pleasant country of Prussian Saxony; and the venerable pile of buildings rising among its meadows, hills, and woods, is worthy of the motto borne on the arms of the old abbey: "*Hier ist nichts anderes denn Gottes Haus, und hier die* Pforte *des Himmels.*"[1] It has a beautifully restored chapel, regular commemorative services, and a host of local usages. A Latin grace is sung in hall every day before dinner by the whole body of scholars. Every scholar has by ancient institution his *tutor*, every master his

[1] "This is none other but the house of God, and this is the gate (*porta, Pforte*) of heaven."—Gen. xxviii. 17.

famulus. This is the German school where Latin verse has been most cultivated, and the *Musæ Portenses*, like those of Eton, have been published. The property is very large, and considerable Church patronage is attached to it. Up to 1815, when it passed into the possession of Prussia, the old abbey estate had still its feudal privileges, and enjoyed full civil and criminal jurisdiction. The property is now entirely under the superintendence of the School Board of the province of Saxony, which appoints a procurator for it. The revenues of Pforta are from £8000 to £9000 a year.

The great head-master of Schulpforta was Ilgen, whose name every one who has read the Homeric Hymns ought to respect. Ilgen was rector for nearly thirty years, from 1802 to 1831; and his reforms make this period an epoch in the school's history. Few schools can show such a list of old scholars. Grævius, Ernesti, Klopstock, Böttiger, Mitscherlich, Fichte, Dissen, Thiersch, Spitzner, Döderlein, Spohn, were all of them schoolboys here.

There are now about 205 pupils: 180 *Alumnen* proper, or collegers, 20 boarders (*Pensionaire, Extraneer*), and four or five half-boarders (*Semi-Ex-*

traneer). These half-boarders have, in fact, all the advantages of collegers, except board, for a payment of £7 : 10s. a year; their board they get at a master's. The real *Extraneer* board and lodge with a master; they pay to him about £45 a year for their board and lodging, and to the school £5 : 8s. a year for their instruction.

The *Alumnen* proper have all of them certain payments to make; those exacted, however, from the 140 who hold *Freistellen* are very trifling. There are 30 old *Koststellen*, or posts with board, the holders of which pay about £3 a year each, and 20 new *Koststellen*, the holders of which pay £7. As a general rule, a boy is not admitted at once to a *Freistelle*. The right of nominating to about half the posts on the foundation belongs to the Crown, that to the other half to different municipalities. Of the Crown appointments a certain number is reserved, by convention with the Saxon Government when Pforta passed into Prussia's possession, for natives of the duchy of Saxony. The rest are given, on grounds of public claim, by the Minister of Justice and the Home Secretary. No boy is admitted till he is twelve years old; he must be able to pass for *tertia*. The school begins with *tertia*, but it has six forms, because there is an upper and a lower division of each class. There are 77 boys in the two divisions of *tertia*, 79 in the two of *secunda*, 49 in the two of *prima*. For some of the posts several boys are nominated, and the one who passes the best examination gets admitted; but the candidates here, the English reader will observe, must all of them be over twelve years of age. The school is well provided with exhibitions, in general of from £10 to £15 a year in value, to the universities.

There is a noteworthy usage here of making one day in the week a *Studientag*, in which the boy is free from all school lessons that he may pursue his private studies. In the same spirit, in the *Gymnasien* generally, promising boys in *prima* are excused certain of the school lessons, that they may work at matters which specially interest them. Results of this private study are to be produced at the *Abiturientenexamen*, and are taken into account for the leaving certificate. Nothing could better show the freedom of Germany, as compared with France, in treating school matters, than a practice of this kind, which to the French authorities would appear monstrous. In England the school authorities would have a belief, in general too well justified, that hardly any one of our boys has any notion of such a thing as systematic private study at all.

At Schulpforta they are very proud of their playing-field, which is indeed, with the wooded hill rising behind it, a pleasant place; but the games of English playing-fields do not go on there: instead of goals or a cricket-ground, one sees apparatus for gymnastics. The Germans, as is well known, now cultivate gymnastics in their schools with great care. Since 1842, gymnastics have been made a regular part of the public-school course; there is a *Central-Turnanstalt* at Berlin, with 18 civilian pupils who are being trained expressly to supply model teachers of gymnastics for the public schools. The teachers profess to have adapted their exercises with precision to every age, and to all the stages of a boy's growth and muscular development. The French are much impressed by what seems to them the success of the Germans in this kind of instruction, and certainly in their own *lycées* they have not at present done nearly so much for it. Nothing, however, will make an ex-schoolboy of one of the great English schools regard the gymnastics of a foreign school without a slight feeling of wonder and compassion, so much more animating and interesting do the games of his remembrance seem to him. This much, however, I will say; if boys have long work-hours, or if they work hard, gymnastics probably do more for their physical health in the comparatively short time allotted to recreation than anything else could. In England the majority of public schoolboys work far less than the foreign schoolboy, and for this majority the English games are delightful; but for the few hard students with us there is in general nothing but the *constitutional*, and this is not so good as the foreign gymnastics. For little boys, again, I am inclined to think that the carefully taught gymnastics of a foreign school are better than the lounging shiveringly about, which in my time used often at our great schools to be the portion of those who had not yet come to full age for games.

All the schools I have hitherto described are

denominational schools. Before I conclude, I must describe a mixed (*simultan*) school, or the nearest approach to it to be found. Such a school is the *Friedrich-Wilhelms Gymnasium* at Cologne. Cologne, as every one knows, is Catholic; up to 1825 it had only one gymnasium, a Catholic one. In 1865 it had two Catholic gymnasiums, one with 382 scholars, the other with 281; it had also a *Realschule* of the first rank, with 601 scholars. Besides these schools it had a Protestant gymnasium, with *real* classes; as we should say, with a modern school forming part of it. This is the *Friedrich-Wilhelms Gymnasium*. An old Carmelite college, which had become the property of the municipality, was in 1825 made into a public gymnasium, in order to relieve the overcrowding in the Catholic gymnasium, and to provide special accommodation for the Protestants. In 1862 this school was, by the subscriptions of friends, both Catholic and Protestant, provided with *real* classes up to *secunda*, the two lowest classes (*sexta* and *quinta*) being common to both classical and *real* scholars. There are, therefore, in fact three special classes for *real* scholars; or as we should say, a modern school of three classes. There are 356 boys in the classical school, and about 100 in the modern school. Of the boys in the classical school, 125 only are Protestants, though the school is by foundation *evangelisch;* 215 are Catholics, and 16 are Jews. Nothing could better show how little the "religious difficulty" practically exists in Prussian schools than this abundance of Catholic scholars in a Protestant school, where the director and the majority of the 15 masters are Protestants. The regular religious instruction of the school is, of course, Protestant; but the Catholics being in such numbers, a special religious instructor has been provided for them, as, too, there is a special religious instructor provided for the Protestants in the two Catholic gymnasiums. It will be remembered that where the boys, not of the confession for which the school is founded, are very few in number, the parents have to make private arrangements for their religious instruction, and the school does not provide it. The school fee is from 18 to 22 thalers a year, according to the form a boy is in.

The property of the school brings in less than £200 a year. The State contributes about £900 a year. School fees produce almost exactly the same sum. The municipality gave in the first instance the school premises, and now contributes about £50 a year to keep them up. It is a Crown patronage school, but the *externa*, or property concerns, of this school, as of all the gymnasiums and school endowments of Cologne, are managed by a local *Verwaltungsrath*, or council of administration. This *Verwaltungsrath* is thus composed: a representative of the Provincial School Board, the directors of the three gymnasiums, with a lawyer, a financier, an administrator, and two citizens of Cologne; these last five chosen, on the presentation of the Common Council, by the Provincial School Board. For the *Studienfonds*, which are endowments general for education in Cologne, and not affected to particular institutions, a Catholic ecclesiastic is added to the *Verwaltungsrath*. These *Studienfonds* are very considerable, producing close upon 60,000 thalers a year (£9000). The *Verwaltungsrath* has a staff of seven clerks, office-keepers, etc., and both council and staff are paid for their services.

The director was the personage already mentioned, whose nomination to a school[1] the Education minister had refused to confirm, because of the nominee's politics. I had much conversation with him, and he struck me as a very able man. He said, and his presence in this Cologne school confirmed it, that the Government found it impossible to treat their school patronage politically, even so far as the directors or head-masters were concerned. The appointment of the professors and teachers, he declared, it never even entered into the Government's head to treat politically. We went through the school admission-book together, that I might see to what class in society the boys chiefly belonged. We took a class in the middle of the school, and went through this boy by boy, both for the classical school and the modern school. As it happened, the social standing of the *real* scholars was on the whole somewhat the highest, but there was very little difference. There were a few peasants' children, picked boys from the elementary schools in the neighbourhood, but these were all of them bursars. There were a good many sons of Government officials. But the designation I found

[1] The school was the gymnasium at Bielefeld.

attached to by far the greater number of parents' names was *Kaufmann*—"trader." I heard several lessons, and particularly noticed the English lesson in the third class of the modern school. This lesson was given by a Swiss, who spoke English very well, and who had been, he told me, a teacher of modern languages at Uppingham. I thought here, as I thought when I heard a French lesson at Bonn, that the boys made a good deal more of these modern language lessons in Germany than in England; the Swiss master at Cologne said this impression of mine was quite right. Even in France I thought these lessons better done,— with better methods, better teachers, and more thoroughly learned,—than in England. In Germany they were better than in France. The lessons in the natural sciences, on the other hand, which in France seemed to me inferior to the mathematical lessons, I thought less successfully given in Germany, than even in France. But of this matter I am a very incompetent judge, and England, besides, supplied me here with no standard of comparison, for in the English schools, when I knew them, the natural sciences were not taught at all. The classical work in the Cologne gymnasium was much the same that I had seen in other Prussian gymnasiums, and calls for no particular remark.

Dr. Jäger, the director of the united school,— well placed, therefore, for judging, and, as I have said, an able man,—assured me it was the universal conviction with those competent to form an opinion that the *Realschulen* were not, at present, successful institutions. He declared that the boys in the corresponding forms of the classical school beat the *Realschule* boys in matters which both do alike, such as history, geography, the mother-tongue, and even French, though to French the *Realschule* boys devote so far more time than their comrades of the classical school. The reason for this, Dr. Jäger affirms, is that the classical training strengthens a boy's mind so much.

This is what, as I have already said, the chief school authorities everywhere in France and Germany testify: I quote Dr. Jäger's testimony in particular, because of his ability and because of his double experience. In Switzerland you do not hear the same story, but the regnant Swiss conception of secondary instruction is, in general, not a liberal but a commercial one; not culture and training of the mind, but what will be of immediate palpable utility in some practical calling, is there the chief matter; and this cannot be admitted as the true scope of secondary instruction. Even in Switzerland, too, there is a talk of introducing Latin into the *Realschule* course, which at present is without it; so impossible is it to follow absolutely the commercial theory of education without finding inconvenience from it. But I reserve my remarks on this question for my conclusion.

CHAPTER VII.

SUPERIOR OR UNIVERSITY INSTRUCTION IN PRUSSIA.

Passage from Secondary to Superior Instruction—Special Schools and Universities—Universities of Prussia—Proportion of University Students to Population—German Universities State Establishments—University Authorities—University Teachers—1. Full Professors—2. Assistant Professors—3. Privatdocenten—Students—Fees—Certificates of Attendance at Lectures—Degrees—The Staatsprüfung—Character of the German University System.

THE secondary school has essentially for its object a general liberal culture, whether this culture is chiefly pursued through the group of aptitudes which carry us to the humanities, or through the group of aptitudes which carry us to the study of nature. It is a mistake to make the secondary school a direct professional school, though a boy's aims in life and his future profession will naturally determine, in the absence of an overpowering bent, the group of aptitudes he will seek to develop. It is the function of the special school to give a professional direction to what a boy has learnt at the secondary school, at the same time that it makes his knowledge, as far as possible, systematic,—develops it into science. It is the function of the university to develop into science the knowledge a boy brings with him from the secondary school, at the same time that it directs him towards the profession in which his knowledge may most naturally be exercised. Thus, in the university, the idea of science is primary, that of the profession secondary; in the special school, the idea of the profession is primary, that of science secondary. Our English special schools have yet to be instituted, and our English universities do not perform the function of a university, as that function is above laid down. Still we have, like Germany, great and famous universities, and those universities are, as in Germany, in immediate connection with our chief secondary schools. It will be well, therefore, to complete my sketch of the Prussian school system by a sketch of the university system with which it is co-ordered.

Prussia had, in 1865, six complete universities, with all the four faculties, of theology, law, medicine, and philosophy; and two incomplete universities, with only the faculties of theology and philosophy. The complete universities were Berlin, Bonn, Breslau, Greifswald, Halle, and Königsberg; the incomplete ones, Münster and Braunsberg. In both of these last the faculty of theology is Catholic.

These eight Prussian universities had, in 1864, 6362 students and 600 professors. But this number does not represent the number of Prussians who come under university instruction, because many Prussians go to German universities out of Prussia, such as Heidelberg, Göttingen, Leipzig, Jena. There is very free circulation of the German students through the universities of the fatherland; and to estimate the proportion, in any German State, who come under superior instruction, the fairest way is to take the proportion which the whole number of students in Germany bears to the whole population. For else, while we get for Prussia but about one student to every 2800 inhabitants, we shall get for Baden, and for the three Saxon duchies, Weimar, Coburg, and

Altenburg, about one student to every 1100 inhabitants; yet it is not that in these territories more of the population go to the university than in Prussia, but Baden has the University of Heidelberg, and the three Saxon duchies have in common the University of Jena, and to these two universities students from all parts of Germany come. Taking, therefore, the whole of Germany, exclusive of the non-German States of Austria, we get about one matriculated student for every 2600 of population; and this proportion is probably pretty near the truth for Prussia, and for most of the single States. In England the proportion is about one matriculated student to every 5800 of the population.

The universities of the several German States differ in many points of detail, but in their main system and regulations they are alike. I shall continue, in speaking of universities, to have Prussia in immediate view; but the English reader will understand that what I say of the Prussian university system may be applied in general to that of all Germany.

The German university is a State establishment, and is maintained, so far as its own resources fall short, by the State. A university's own resources are both the property it has and the fees it levies. The two most important of the Prussian universities, Berlin with its 2500 students and Bonn with its 1000, date from this century, and foundations of this century are seldom very rich in property. For the year 1864, the income of the University of Berlin was 196,787 thalers (£29,518); of this sum, the real and funded property of the university produced 161 thalers, fees produced 7557 thalers. The State gave all the rest,—189,069 thalers (about £28,842). And the State which does this is the most frugal and economical State in Europe.

The Minister of Public Instruction appoints the professors of a university, the academical senate having the right of proposing names for his acceptance; and he has also his representative in each university,—the *curator*,—who acts as plenipotentiary for the State, and whose business it is to see to the observance of the laws and regulations which concern the universities. Thus, for instance, a full professor (*Professor ordinarius*) is bound by regulation to give throughout the *Semester*, or half-year, at least two free lectures a week on his subject; if he tried to charge fees for them, it would be the curator's business to interfere. And the university authorities cannot make new regulations for the government of the university without obtaining for them the sanction of the minister and of Parliament. Still the university authorities practically work, in Germany just as much as in this country, their own university; the real direction of the university is in their hands, and not, as in France, in those of the minister.

These university authorities are the following. First comes the rector, or, in cases where the sovereign is the titular rector, as at Halle and Jena, the pro-rector, who answers to our vice-chancellor; only he is elected for one year only, instead of four. His electors are the full professors. The rector or pro-rector is the visible head of the university, and is charged with its discipline. Like our vice-chancellor, he has an assessor, or judge, who sits with him whenever there is a question of inflicting fines, or whenever one of the parties appearing before him is not a member of the university. The academical senate is also chosen by the full professors, and for one year; its members consisting of the actual rector (or pro-rector), the outgoing rector, and a full professor of each faculty. In some universities all the full professors are members of the academical senate. The rector is president, and the internal affairs of the university are brought before it for its discussion and regulation.

Next come the faculties. The faculties in nearly all German universities are four in number:[1] theology, law, medicine, and philosophy. Philosophy embraces the humanities, and the mathematical and natural sciences. As a university authority, a faculty consists only of its full professors, headed by the dean, whom these professors elect for one year. It is the business of the faculty thus composed to see that the students attend regularly the courses of lectures for which they are entered, to summon defaulters before it, to reprimand them, and to inflict on them, if it think proper, a slight penalty.

[1] In one or two universities there is a separate faculty for political economy ; in general this science is comprehended in the faculty of philosophy.

The last university authority to be mentioned is the *quæstor*. He has to collect from the students the fees for the courses for which they have entered themselves, and to pay those fees to the professors to whom they are due, a small deduction being made for the quæstor's salary and for the university chest.

And now to take the university, not as an administrative but as a teaching body. Of the university, considered in this capacity, the *faculty* is a very different thing from the limited faculty above described. The university faculty, as a teaching body, comprehends not only all the full professors of that faculty, but all its professors extraordinary, or assistant professors, and all its *Privatdocenten*. The dean of faculty ascertains from all the full professors, all the professors extraordinary, and all the *Privatdocenten* of his faculty, what subject each one of them proposes to treat in the coming *Semester*: there is perfect liberty of choice for each lecturer, but by consent among themselves they so co-order their teaching that the whole field of instruction proper to their faculty may be completely covered.

Then the dean calls together the full professors, who make the administrative faculty; and the programme of lectures is by them drawn up from the data collected by the dean, and is promulgated by their authority.

All full professors must have the degree of doctor in their faculty. Each of them is named for a special branch of the instruction of his faculty; and in this branch he is bound, as I have said, to give at least two public lectures a week without charging fees. He receives from the State a fixed salary, which is sometimes as much as £350 or even £400 a year; he has also a share in the examination fees, and he has the fees for what lectures he gives besides his public lectures. The regular number of full professors in each university is limited, but the State can always, if it thinks fit, nominate an eminent man as full professor in a faculty, even though the faculty may have its complement of full professors; and the State then pays him the same salary as the other full professors. Both from the consideration which attaches to the post and from its emolument, a full professor's place is in Germany the prize of the career of public instruction, and no schoolmaster's place can compare with it. At Heidelberg several professors have, I am told, an income, from fixed salary and fees together, of £1000 a year, and one an income of £1500.

The professors extraordinary, or assistant professors, are also named by the State, but they have not in all cases a fixed salary. Their main dependence is on fees paid by those who come to their lectures. They are in general taken from the most distinguished of the *Privatdocenten*, and they rise through the post of professor extraordinary to that of full professor.

Other countries have full professors and professors extraordinary. France, for instance, has her *professeurs titulaires*, and her *professeurs suppléants;* but the *Privatdocent* is peculiar to Germany, and is the great source of vigour and renovation to her superior instruction. Sometimes he gives private lessons, like the private tutors of our universities; these lessons have the title of *Privatissima*. But this is not his main business. His main business is as unlike the sterile business of our private tutors as possible. The *Privatdocent* is an assistant to the professorate; he is free to use, when the professors do not occupy them, the university lecture-rooms, he gives lectures like the professors, and his lectures count as professors' lectures for those who attend them. His appointment is on this wise. A distinguished student applies to be made *Privatdocent* in a faculty. He produces certain certificates and performs certain exercises before two delegates named by the faculty, and this is called his *Habilitation*. If he passes, the faculty names him *Privatdocent*. The authorisation of the minister is also requisite for him, but this follows his nomination by the faculty as a matter of course. He is then free to lecture on any of the matters proper to his faculty. He is on his probation, he receives no salary whatever, and depends entirely on his lectures; he has, therefore, every motive to exert himself. In general, as I have said, the professors and *Privatdocenten* arrange together to parcel out the field of instruction between them, and one supplements the other's teaching; still a *Privatdocent* may, if he likes, lecture on just the same subject that a professor is lecturing on; there is absolute liberty in this respect. The one precaution taken against undue competition is, that a *Privatdocent* lecturing on a professor's subject is not allowed to charge lower fees than the professor. It does honour to the disinterested spirit in which science is pursued in Germany, that with these temptations to competition the relations between the professors and the *Privatdocenten* are in general excellent; the distinguished professor encourages the rising *Privatdocent,* and the *Privatdocent* seeks to make his teaching serve science, not his own vanity. But it is evident how the neighbourhood of a rising young *Privatdocent* must tend to keep a professor up to the mark, and hinder him from getting sleepy and lazy. If he gets sleepy and lazy, his lecture-room is deserted. The *Privatdocent,* again, has the standard of eminent men before his eyes, and everything stimulates him to come up to it.

In the faculty of philosophy at Berlin the number of *Privatdocenten* is almost exactly the same as the number of full professors. There are 28 full professors and 29 *Privatdocenten.* The professors extraordinary are more numerous than either. They are 33 in number. The whole number of teachers in the University of Berlin is 183.[1]

Now I come to the students. The university course in theology, law, and philosophy takes three years; in medicine it takes four or five. A student in his *triennium* often visits one or two universities, seldom more. Lachmann (to take an eminent instance) first went for half a year to Leipzig to hear Hermann; then he passed on to Göttingen, where he afterwards got his *Habilitation.* To become a member of a university, the student has to be entered on the university register (*Matrikel*), and then on the register of the faculty in which he means to follow lectures ; for inscription on the university register the production of the school-leaving certificate (*Maturitätszeugniss*), of which I have already said so much, is indispensable. You may get leave to

---

[1] All these numbers relate to the year 1864. For full details respecting the provision of teaching in the University of Berlin, see the Appendix.

attend lectures without being a member of the university, and without any school certificate; but such attendance counts nothing for any purpose for which a university course is by law or official rule required. The university entrance fee is about 18s. The matriculating student signs an engagement to observe the laws and regulations of the university. The penalties for violating them are enforced by the rector. These penalties are, according to the nature of the offence, reprimand; fine; imprisonment for a period not exceeding one month in the university *carcer; consilium abeundi*, or dismissal from the particular university to which the student belongs, but with liberty to enter at another; and finally, *Relegation*, or absolute expulsion, notice being sent to the other universities, which then may not admit the student expelled.

The lecture fees range from 16s. to £1 : 14s. for every course which is not a public and gratuitous one. They are somewhat higher at Berlin than in most German universities. In the faculty of medicine they are highest; here they go up as high as £1 : 14s. a *Semester* for a course of about five hours a week. A course of the same length in theology or philosophy costs at Berlin about 17s. a *Semester*. The fees are collected, as I have said, by the university quæstor, and they must be paid in advance. But every professor has the power to admit poor auditors to his lectures without fee, and often he does so. Poor students are also, by a humane arrangement, suffered to attend lectures on credit, and afterwards, when they enter the public service,—which in Prussia means not only what we in England call the public service, but the learned professions as well, —their lecture fees are recovered by a deduction from their salary. Each university has besides, for the benefit of poor scholars, a number of exhibitions ranging from £12 to £60 a year; and it is common to allow the holders of school exhibitions—which are of smaller amount, and range from £6 to £30 a year,—to retain them at the university.

Certificates of having followed certain courses of lectures are required both for the university degree and for the subsequent examination for a public career (*Staatsprüfung*) which almost every university student has in view. It is said that the professors whose lectures are very numerously attended have difficulty in ascertaining who is there and who is not, and that they give the certificates with too much laxity. In general, however, it is certain that a student who has his way to make, and who is worth anything, will attend regularly the lectures for which he has entered himself and paid his money. There are, of course, many idlers; the proportion of students in a German university who really work I have heard estimated at one-third; certainly it is larger than in the English universities. But the pressure put upon them in the way of compulsion and university examinations is much less than with us. The paramount university aim in Germany is to encourage a love of study and science for their own sakes; and the professors, very unlike our college tutors, are constantly warning their pupils against *Brodstudien*, studies pursued with a view to examinations and posts. The examinations within the university course itself are far fewer and less important in Germany than in England. It is Austria, a country which believes in the things of the mind as little as we do, which is the great country for university examinations. There they are applied with a mechanical faith much like ours, and come as often as once a month; but the general intellectual life of the Austrian universities is lower, though Vienna and Prague are good medical schools, than that of any other universities of Germany. "Le pays à examens, l'Autriche,"—exclaims an eminent French professor, M. Laboulaye, who has carefully studied the German university system with a view to reforming that of France,— "Le pays à examens, l'Autriche, est précisément celui dans lequel on ne travaille pas;" and every competent authority in Germany will confirm what M. Laboulaye says. I do not say that in countries like Austria and England, where there is so little real love for the things of the mind, examinations may not be a protection from something worse.[1] All I say is that a love for the things of the mind is what we want, and that examinations will never give it.

---

[1] Although I am no very ardent lover of examinations, I am inclined to think the non-Austrian universities of Germany might with advantage make a somewhat greater use of them.

Each faculty in a German university examines for degrees in that faculty and confers them. The *Maturitätszeugniss* which the student brings with him from school answers to our grade of bachelor of arts. The degree of licentiate, answering to our degree of master, is only given in theology and philosophy, and is not often sought for. The great faculty degree is the degree of doctor. For this a certificate of university studies, an oral examination, and a written dissertation, are required. The dissertation is in Latin or German, and is usually published. A doctor's degree in philosophy costs £17 at Berlin; there are faculties and universities in which a doctor's degree costs as much as £22 : 10s. A poor student who passes a brilliant examination has sometimes his degree given him without fees. I have already said that the degree of doctor is given much more easily and carelessly in some German universities than in others. But in none is the degree examination in itself such as to make it what the degree examination is with us—the grand final cause of the university life. "Der Zweck des Lebens ist das Leben selbst," says the German poet; and this is certainly true, in Germany, of the university life.

The *Staatsprüfung*, however, supplies a bracing examination test; but this examination falls outside the sphere of the university itself. As I have again and again begged the English reader to remark, the examination test is never used in Prussia as sufficient in itself; it is only used to make the assurance of a really good education doubly sure; the really good education is regarded as the main assurance, and no one who has not had this may present himself for the *Staatsprüfung*. The student who leaves a university receives from the rector a certificate mentioning what lectures he has attended, and what the character of his university career has been. With this certificate, and with the leaving certificate of his school, the future civil servant, clergyman, lawyer, or doctor, presents himself before an examining commission (*Prüfungscommission*) such as I have described in an earlier part of this volume. He is then examined, having three or four days of paper work, and six or eight hours of *vivâ voce*. For lawyers and for clergymen there is a double examination, the second coming three years after the first.

Such, sketched in the briefest possible outline, is the system of the German universities. *Lehrfreiheit* and *Lernfreiheit*, liberty for the teacher and liberty for the learner; and *Wissenschaft*, science, knowledge systematically pursued and prized in and for itself, are the fundamental ideas of that system. The French, with their ministerial programmes for superior instruction, and their ministerial authorisations required for any one who wants to give a course of public lectures,—authorisations which are by no means a matter of form,—are naturally most struck with the liberty of the German universities, and it is in liberty that they have most need to borrow from them. To us, ministerial programmes and ministerial authorisations are unknown; our university system is a routine, indeed, but it is our want of science, not our want of liberty, which makes it a routine. It is in science that we have most need to borrow from the German universities. The French university has no liberty, and the English universities have no science; the German universities have both.

CHAPTER VIII.

GENERAL CONCLUSION. SCHOOL STUDIES.

Probable Issue of the Conflict between Classical and Real Studies —New Conception of the Aim and Office of Instruction— The Circle of Knowledge takes in both the Humanities and the Study of Nature—This not enough recognised at present—Tyranny of the Humanists—Tyranny of the Realists —Our present School Course—How to Transform it—Excessive Preponderance of Grammatical Studies, and of Latin and Greek Composition—The Ancient Languages to be more Studied as Literature—And the Modern Languages likewise —Summing up of Conclusions.

IN what has been said, two points, above all, suggest matter for reflection: the course of study of foreign schools, and the way in which these schools are established and administered. I begin with the first.

Several times in the foregoing chapters I have touched upon the conflict between the gymnasium and the *Realschule*, between the partisans of the old classical studies and the partisans of what are called real, or modern, or useful studies. This conflict is not yet settled, either by one side crushing the other by mere violence, or by one side clearly getting the best of the other in the dispute between them. We in England, behindhand as our public instruction in many respects is, are nevertheless in time to profit, and to make our schools profit, by the solution which will certainly be found for this difference. I am inclined to think that both sides will, as is natural, have to abate their extreme pretensions. The modern spirit tends to reach a new conception of the aim and office of instruction; when this conception is fully reached, it will put an end to conflict, and will probably show both the humanists and the realists to have been right in their main ideas.

The aim and office of instruction, say many people, is to make a man a good citizen, or a good Christian or a gentleman; or it is to fit him to get on in the world, or it is to enable him to do his duty in that state of life to which he is called. It is none of these, and the modern spirit more and more discerns it to be none of these. These are at best secondary and indirect aims of instruction; its prime direct aim is to enable a man *to know himself and the world.* Such knowledge is the only sure basis for action, and this basis it is the true aim and office of instruction to supply. To know himself, a man must know the capabilities and performances of the human spirit; and the value of the humanities, of *Alterthumswissenschaft,* the science of antiquity, is, that it affords for this purpose an unsurpassed source of light and stimulus. Whoever seeks help for knowing himself from knowing the capabilities and performances of the human spirit will nowhere find a more fruitful object of study than in the achievements of Greece in literature and the arts during the two centuries from the birth of Simonides to the death of Plato. And these two centuries are but the flowering-point of a long period, during the whole of which the ancient world offers, to the student of the capabilities and performances of the human spirit, lessons of capital importance.

This the humanists have perceived, and the truth of this perception of theirs is the stronghold of their position. It is a vital and formative knowledge to know the most powerful manifestations of the human spirit's activity, for the knowledge of them greatly feeds and quickens our own activity; and they are very imperfectly known without knowing ancient Greece and Rome. But it is also a vital and formative knowledge to know the world, the laws which govern nature, and man as a part of nature. This the realists have perceived, and the truth of this perception, too, is inexpugnable. Every man is born with aptitudes which give him access to vital and formative knowledge by one of these roads; either by the road of studying man and his works, or by the road of studying nature and her works. The business of instruction is to seize and develop these aptitudes. The great and complete spirits which have all the aptitudes for both roads of knowledge are rare. But much more might be done on both roads by the same mind, if instruction clearly grasped the idea of the entire system of aptitudes for which it has to provide; of their correlation, and of their *equipollency*, so to speak, as all leading, if rightly employed, to vital knowledge; and if then, having grasped this idea, it provided for them. The Greek spirit, after its splendid hour of creative activity was gone, gave our race another precious lesson, by exhibiting in the career of men like Aristotle and the great students of Alexandria, this idea of the correlation and equal dignity of the most different departments of human knowledge, and by showing the possibility of uniting them in a single mind's education. A man like Eratosthenes is memorable by what he performed, but still more memorable by his commanding range of studies, and by the broad basis of culture out of which his performances grew. As our public instruction gets a clearer view of its own functions, of the relations of the human spirit to knowledge, and of the entire circle of knowledge, it will certainly more learn to awaken in its pupils an interest in that entire circle, and less allow them to remain total strangers to any part of it. Still, the circle is so vast and human faculties are so limited, that it is for the most part through a single aptitude, or group of aptitudes, that each individual will really get his access to intellectual life and vital knowledge; and it is by effectually directing these aptitudes on definite points of the circle, that he will really obtain his comprehension of the whole.

Meanwhile, neither our humanists nor our realists adequately conceive the circle of knowledge, and each party is unjust to all that to which its own aptitudes do not carry it. The humanists are loath to believe that man has any access to vital knowledge except by knowing himself, — the poetry, philosophy, history, which his spirit has created; the realists, that he has any access except by knowing the world,—the physical sciences, the phenomena and laws of nature. I, like so many others who have been brought up in the old routine, imperfectly as I know letters,— the work of the human spirit itself,—know nothing else, and my judgment therefore may fairly be impeached. But it seems to me that so long as the realists persist in cutting in two the circle of knowledge, so long do they leave for practical purposes the better portion to their rivals, and in the government of human affairs their rivals will beat them. And for this reason. The study of letters is the study of the operation of human force, of human freedom and activity; the study of nature is the study of the operation of non-human forces, of human limitation and passivity. The contemplation of human force and activity tends naturally to heighten our own force and activity; the contemplation of human limits and passivity tends rather to check it. Therefore the men who have had the humanistic training have played, and yet play, so prominent a part in human affairs, in spite of their prodigious ignorance of the universe; because their training has powerfully fomented the human force in them. And in this way letters are indeed *runes*, like those magic runes taught by the Valkyrie Brynhild to Sigurd, the Scandinavian Achilles, which put the crown to his endowment and made him invincible.

Still, the humanists themselves suffer so much from the ignorance of physical facts and laws, and from the inadequate conception of nature, and of man as a part of nature,—the conduct of human affairs suffers so much from the same cause,—that the intellectual insufficiency of the humanities, conceived as the one access to vital knowledge, is perhaps at the present moment yet more striking than their power of practical stimulation; and we may willingly declare with the Italians[1] that no part of the circle of knowledge is common or unclean, none is to be cried up at the expense of another. To say that the fruit of classics, in the boys who study them, is at present greater than the fruit of the natural sciences, to say that the realists have not got their matters of instruction so well adapted to teaching purposes as the humanists have got theirs, comes really to no more than this: that the realists are but newly admitted labourers in the field of practical instruction, and that while the leading humanists, the Wolfs and the Buttmanns, have been also schoolmasters, and have brought their mind and energy to bear upon the school-teaching of their own studies, the leaders in the natural sciences, the Davys and the Faradays, have not. When scientific physics have as recognised a place in public instruction as Latin and Greek, they will be as well taught.

[1] "Essendo diverse le parti dell insegnamento, nessuno mostri di spregiare le altre, esaltando troppo quella cui è addetto. Nessun ramo del sapere è meno necessario ; di tutte le scienze si avvantaggia l'umana società ; tutte cospirano al suo bene."—MATTEUCCI.

The Abbé Fleury, than whom no man is a better authority, says of the mediæval universities, the parents of our public secondary schools: "Les universités ont eu le malheur de commencer dans un temps où le goût des bonnes études était perdu." They were too late for the influences of the great time of Christian literature and eloquence, the first five centuries after Christ; they were even too late for the influences of the time of Abelard and Saint Bernard. And Fleury adds: "De là (from these universities founded in a time of inferior insight) nous est venu ce cours réglé d'études qui subsiste encore." He wrote this in 1708, but it is in the main still true in 1867. All the historical part of this volume has shown that the great movements of the human spirit have either not got hold of the public schools, or not kept hold of them. What reforms have been made have been patchwork, the work of able men who into certain departments of school study which were dear to them infused reality and life, but who looked little beyond these departments, and did not concern themselves with fully adjusting instruction to

M

the wants of the human mind. There is, therefore, no intelligent tradition to be set aside in our public schools; there is only a routine, arising in the way we have seen, and destined to be superseded as soon as ever that more adequate idea of instruction, of which the modern spirit is even now in travail, shall be fully born.

That idea, so far as one can already forecast its lineaments, will subordinate the matter and methods of instruction to the end in view; the end of conducting the pupil, as I have said, through the means of his special aptitudes, to a knowledge of himself and the world. The natural sciences are a necessary instrument of this knowledge; letters and *Alterthumswissenschaft* are a necessary instrument of this knowledge. But if school instruction in the natural sciences has almost to be created, school instruction in letters and *Alterthumswissenschaft* has almost to be created anew. The prolonged philological discipline, which in our present schools guards the access to *Alterthumswissenschaft*, brings to mind the philosophy of Albertus Magnus, the mere introduction to which,—the logic,— was by itself enough to absorb all a student's time of study. To combine the philological discipline with the matter to which it is ancillary,—with *Alterthumswissenschaft* itself,—a student must be of the force of Wolf, who used to sit up the whole night with his feet in a tub of cold water and one of his eyes bound up to rest while he read with the other, and who thus managed to get through all the Greek and Latin classics at school, and also Scapula's Lexicon and Faber's Thesaurus; and who at Göttingen would sweep clean out of the library-shelves all the books illustrative of the classic on which Heyne was going to lecture, and finish them in a week. Such students are rare; and nine out of ten, especially in England, where so much time is given to Greek and Latin composition, never get through the philological vestibule at all, never arrive at *Alterthumswissenschaft*, which is a knowledge of the spirit and power of Greek and Roman antiquity learned from its original works.

But many people have even convinced themselves that the preliminary philological discipline is so extremely valuable as to be an end in itself; and, similarly, that the mathematical discipline preliminary to a knowledge of nature is so extremely valuable as to be an end in itself. It seems to me that those who profess this conviction do not enough consider the quantity of knowledge inviting the human mind, and the importance to the human mind of really getting to it. No preliminary discipline is to be pressed at the risk of keeping minds from getting at the main matter, a knowledge of themselves and the world. Some minds have such a special aptitude for philology, or for pure mathematics, that their access to vital knowledge and their genuine intellectual life lies in and through those studies; but for one whose natural access to vital knowledge is by these paths, there will be ten whose natural access to it is through literature, philosophy, history, or through some one or more of the natural sciences. No doubt it is indispensable to have exact habits of mind, and mathematics and grammar are excellent for the promotion of these habits; and Latin, besides having so large a share in so many modern languages, offers a grammar which is the best of all grammars for the purpose of this promotion. Here are valid reasons for making every schoolboy learn some Latin and some mathematics, but not for turning the preliminary matter into the principal, and sacrificing every aptitude except that for the science of language or of pure mathematics. A Latin grammar of thirty pages, and the most elementary treatise of arithmetic and of geometry, would amply suffice for the uses of philology and mathematics as a universally imposed preparatory discipline. By keeping within these strict limits, absolute exactness of knowledge,—the habit which is here our professed aim,—might be far better attained than it is at present. But it is well to insist, besides, that all knowledge may and should, when we have got fit teachers for it, be so taught as to promote exact habits of mind; and we are not to take leave of these when we pass beyond our introductory discipline.

But it is sometimes said that only through close philological studies and the close practice of Greek and Latin composition can *Alterthums-wissenschaft* itself, the science of the ancient world, be truly reached. It is said to be only through these that we get really to know Greek and Latin literature. For all practical purposes this proposition is untrue, and its untruth may be easily tested. Ask a good Greek scholar, in the ordinary English acceptation of that term, who at the same time knows a modern literature,—let us say the French literature,—well, whether he feels himself to have most seized the spirit and power of French literature or of Greek literature. Undoubtedly he has most seized the spirit and power of French literature, simply because he has read so very much more of it. But if, instead of reading work after work of French literature, he had read only a few works or parts of works in it, and had given the rest of his time for study to the sedulous practice of French composition, and to minutely learning the structure and laws of the French language, then he would know the French literature much as he knows the Greek; he might write very creditable French verses, but he would have seized the spirit and power of French literature not half so much as he has seized them at present. No doubt it is well to know French philology like M. Littré, and to know French literature too; or to write Italian verse like Arthur Hallam, and to know Italian literature too ; just as it is well to know the Greek lexicographers and grammarians as Wolf did, and yet to know, also, Greek literature in its length and breadth. But it needs a very rare student for this : and, as, if an Englishman is to choose between writing Italian sonnets and knowing Italian literature, it is better for him to know Italian literature, so, if he is to choose between writing Greek iambics and knowing Greek literature, it is better for him to know Greek literature. But an immense development of grammatical studies, and an immense use of Latin and Greek composition, take so much of the pupil's time, that in nine cases out of ten he has not any sense at all of Greek and Latin literature as *literature*, and ends his studies without getting any. His verbal scholarship and his composition he is pretty sure in after life to drop, and then all his Greek and Latin is lost. Greek and Latin *literature*, if he had ever caught the notion of them, would have been far more likely to stick by him.

I was myself brought up in the straitest school of Latin and Greek composition, and am certainly not disposed to be unjust to them. Very often they are ignorantly disparaged. Professor Ritschl, I am told, envies the English schools their Latin verse, and he is no bad judge of what is useful for knowing Latin. The close appropriation of the models, which is necessary for good Latin or Greek composition, not only conduces to accurate and verbal scholarship ; it may beget, besides, an intimate sense of those models, which makes us sharers of their spirit and power; and this is of the essence of true *Alterthumswissenschaft*. Herein lies the reason for giving boys more of Latin composition than of Greek, superior though the Greek literature be to the Latin; but the power of the Latin classic is in *character*, that of the Greek is in *beauty*. Now, character is capable of being taught, learnt, and assimilated; beauty hardly ; and it is for enabling us to learn and catch some *power* of antiquity, that Greek or Latin composition is most to be valued. Who shall say what share the turning over and over in their mind, and masticating, so to speak, in early life as models of their Latin verse, such things as Virgil's

"Disce, puer, virtutem ex me, verumque laborem"—

or Horace's

"Fortuna sævo læta negotio"—

has not had in forming the high spirit of the upper class in France and England, the two countries where Latin verse has most ruled the schools, and the two countries which most have had, or have, a high upper class and a high upper class spirit? All this is no doubt to be considered when we are judging the worth of the old school training.

But, in the first place, dignity and a high spirit is not all, or half all, that is to be got out of *Alterthumswissenschaft*. What else is to be got out of it,—the love of the things of the mind, the flexibility, the spiritual moderation,—is for our present time and needs still more precious, and our upper class suffers greatly by not having got it. In the second place, though I do not deny that there are persons with such eminent aptitudes for Latin and Greek composition that they may be brought in contact with the spirit and power of *Alterthumswissenschaft*, and thus with vital knowledge, through them,—as neither do I deny that there are persons with such eminent aptitudes for grammatical and philological studies, that they may be brought in contact with vital knowledge through *them*,—nevertheless, I am convinced that of the hundreds whom our present system tries without distinction to bring into contact with *Alterthumswissenschaft* through composition and philology almost alone, the immense majority would have a far better chance of being brought into vital contact with it through literature, by treating the study of Greek and Latin as we treat our French, or Italian, or German studies. In other words, the number of persons with aptitudes for being carried to vital knowledge by the literary, or historical, or philosophical, or artistic sense,—to each of which senses we give a chance by treating Greek and Latin as literature, and not as mere scholarship,—is infinitely greater than the number of those whose aptitudes are for composition and philology.[1]

I cannot help thinking, therefore, that the modern

---

[1] Since the above remarks were in print they have received powerful corroboration from the eminent authority of Mr. Mill, in his inaugural address at St. Andrews. The difference of my conclusions on one or two points from Mr. Mill's only makes the general coincidence of view more conspicuous; Mr. Mill having been conducted to this view by independent reflection, and I by

spirit will deprive Latin and Greek composition and verbal scholarship of their present universal and preponderant application in our secondary schools, and will make them, as practised on their present high scale, *Privatstudien*, as the Germans say, for boys with an eminent aptitude for them. For the mass of boys the Latin and Greek composition will be limited, as we now limit our French, Italian, and German composition, to the exercises of translation auxiliary to acquiring any language soundly; and the verbal scholarship will be limited to learning the elementary grammar and common forms and laws of the language with a thoroughness which cannot be too exact, and which may easily be more exact than that which we now attain with our much more ambitious grammatical studies. A far greater quantity of Latin and Greek literature might, with the time thus saved, be read, and in a far more interesting

observation of the foreign schools and of the movement of ideas on the Continent.

A very interesting lecture from Mr. Farrar has still more recently come to show us this movement of ideas extending itself to the schools of England, and to distinguished teachers in the most distinguished of these schools.

manner. With the Latin and Greek classics, too, might be joined, as a part of the literary and humanistic course for those whose aptitude is in this direction, a great deal more of the classics of the chief modern languages than we have time for with our present system.

We have still to make the mother-tongue and its literature a part of the school course; foreign nations have done this, and we shall do it; but neither foreign nations nor we have yet quite learnt how to deal, for school purposes, with modern foreign languages. The great notion is to teach them for speaking purposes, with a view to practical convenience. This notion clearly belongs to what I have called the commercial theory of education, and not the liberal theory; and the faultiness of the commercial theory is well seen by examining this notion and its fruits. Mr. Marsh, the well-known author of the *History of the English Language*, who has passed his life in diplomacy and is himself at once a *savant* and a linguist, told me he had been much struck by remarking how, in general, the accomplishment of speaking foreign languages tends to strain the mind, and to make it superficial and averse to going deep in anything. He instanced the young diplomatists of the new school, who, he said, could rattle along in two or three languages, but could do nothing else. Perhaps in old times the young diplomatists could neither do that nor anything else, so in their case there may be now a gain; but there is great truth in Mr. Marsh's remark that the speaking several languages tends to make the thought thin and shallow, and so far from in itself carrying us to vital knowledge, needs a compensating force to prevent its carrying us away from it. But the true aim of schools and instruction is to develop the powers of our mind and to give us access to vital knowledge.

Again : if the speaking of foreign languages is a prime school aim, this aim is clearly best reached by sending a boy to a foreign school. Great numbers of English parents, accordingly, who from their own want of culture are particularly prone to the more obvious theory of education,— the commercial one,— send their boys abroad to be educated. Yet the basis of character and aptitudes proper for living and working in any country is no doubt best formed by being reared in that country, and passing the ductile and susceptible time of boyhood there; and in this case Solomon's saying applies admirably: "*As a bird that wandereth from her nest, so is a man that wandereth from his place.*" That, therefore, can hardly be a prime school-aim, which to be duly reached requires from the scholar an almost irreparable sacrifice. So the learning to speak foreign languages, showy as the accomplishment always is, and useful as it often is, must be regarded as a quite secondary and subordinate school-aim. Something of it may be naturally got in connection with learning the languages; and, above all, the instructor's precept and practice in pronunciation should be sound, not, as in our old way of teaching these languages through incompetent English masters it too often was, utterly barbarous and misleading; but all this part is to be perfected elsewhere, and is not to be looked upon as true school business. It is as literature, and as opening fresh roads into knowledge, that the modern foreign languages, like the ancient, are truly school business; and far more ought to be done with them, on this view of their use, than has ever been done yet.

To sum up, then, the conclusions to which these remarks lead. The ideal of a general, liberal training, is to carry us to a knowledge of ourselves and the world. We are called to this knowledge by special aptitudes which are born with us; the grand thing in teaching is to have faith that some aptitudes of this kind every one has. This one's special aptitudes are for knowing men,—the study of the humanities; that one's special aptitudes are for knowing the world—the study of nature. The circle of knowledge comprehends both, and we should all have some notion, at any rate, of the whole circle of knowledge. The rejection of the humanities by the realists, the rejection of the study of nature by the humanists, are alike ignorant. He whose aptitudes carry him to the study of nature should have some notion of the humanities; he whose aptitudes carry him to the humanities should have some notion of the phenomena and laws of nature. Evidently, therefore, the beginnings of a liberal culture should be the same for both. The mother-tongue, the elements of Latin and of the chief modern languages, the elements of history, of arithmetic and geometry, of geography, and of the knowledge of nature, should be the studies of the lower classes in all secondary schools, and should be the same for all boys at this stage. So far, therefore, there is no reason for a division of schools. But then comes a *bifurcation*, according to the boy's aptitudes and aims. Either the study of the humanities or the study of nature is henceforth to be the predominating part of his instruction. Evidently there are some advantages in making one school include those who follow both these studies. It is the more economical arrangement; and when the humanistic and the real studies are in the same school there is less likelihood of the social stamp put on the boy following the one of them being different from that put on a boy following the other. Still the *bifurcation* within one school, as practised in France, did not answer. But I think this was because the character of the one school remained so overwhelmingly humanistic, because the humanist body of teachers was in general much superior to the realist body, and because the claims of the humanities were allowed to pursue a boy so jealously into his *real* studies. In my opinion, a clever *Realschuler*, who has gone properly through the general grounding of the lower classes, is likely to develop the greater taste for the humanities the more he is suffered to follow his *real* studies without let or stint. The ideal place of instruction would be, I think, one where in the upper classes (the instruction in the lower classes having been the same for all scholars) both humanistic and *real* studies were as judiciously prosecuted, with as good teaching and with as generous a consideration for the main aptitudes of the pupil, as the different branches of humanistic study are now prosecuted in the best German *Gymnasien;* where an attempt is certainly made, by exempting a pupil from lessons not in the direction of his aptitudes, and by encouraging and guiding him to develop these through *Privatstudien*, to break through that Procrustean routine which after a certain point is the bane of great schools. There should, after a certain point, be no cast-iron course for all scholars, either in humanistic or naturalistic studies. According to his aptitude, the pupil should be suffered to follow principally one branch of either of the two great lines of study; and, above all, to interchange the lines occasionally, following, on the line which is not his own line, such studies as have yet some connection with his own line or, from any cause whatever, some attraction for him. He cannot so well do this if the *Gymnasium* and the *Realschule* are two totally separate schools.

His doing it at all, however, is, it will be said, only an ideal. True, but it is an ideal which the modern spirit is, more and more, casting about to realise. To realise it fully, the main thing needful is, first, a clear central conception of what one can and should do by instruction. It is, secondly, a body of teachers in all the branches of each of the two main lines of study, thoroughly masters of their business, and of whom every man shall be set to teach that branch which he has thoroughly mastered, and shall not be allowed to teach any that he has not.

CHAPTER IX.

GENERAL CONCLUSION CONTINUED. SCHOOL ESTABLISHMENT.

England and the Continent—Civil Organisation in Modern States—Civil Organisation Transformed not only in France but also in other Continental States—Not in England—A result of this in English Popular Education—English Secondary and Superior Instruction not touched by the State—Inconveniences of this—The Social Inconvenience—The Intellectual Inconvenience—Their Practical Results—Science and Systematic Knowledge more prized on the Continent than in England—Effect of this on our Application of the Sciences, and on our Schools and Education in General—A better Organisation of Secondary and Superior Instruction a Remedy for our Deficiencies—Public and Private Schools—Necessity for Public Schools—With Public Schools, an Education Minister necessary—A High Council of Education desirable—Functions of such a Council—Provincial School Boards requisite—How to make Public Schools—Defects of our University System—Oxford and Cambridge merely *Hauts Lycées*—London University merely a Board of Examiners—Insufficient number of Students under Superior Instruction in England—Special

Schools wanted, and a Reorganised University System, taking Superior Instruction to the Students, and not bringing these Students to Oxford and Cambridge for it—Centres of Superior Instruction to be formed in different parts of England, and Professors to be organised in Faculties—Oxford, Cambridge, and London to remain the only Degree-Granting Bodies—Education Minister should have the Appointment of Professors—Probable Co-operation of existing Bodies with the State in organising this New Superior Instruction—How, when established, it should be employed—Final Conclusion.

I COME next to the second point for consideration: the mode of establishing and administering schools. I have now on two occasions, first in 1859, and again in 1865, had to make a close study, on the spot and for many months together, of one of the most important branches of the civil organisation of the most civilised States of the Continent. Few Englishmen have had such an experience. If the convictions with which it leaves me seem strange to many Englishmen, it is not that I am differently constituted from the rest of my countrymen, but that I have seen what would certainly give to them too, if they had seen it with their own eyes as I have, reflections which they never had before. No one of open mind, and not hardened in routine and prejudice, could observe for so long and from so near as I observed it, the civil organisation of France, Germany, Italy, Switzerland, Holland, without having the conviction forced upon him that these countries have a civil organisation which has been framed with forethought and design to meet the wants of modern society; while our civil organisation in England still remains what time and chance have made it. The States which we really resemble, in this respect, are Austria and Rome. I remember I had the honour of saying to Cardinal Antonelli, when he asked me what I thought of the Roman schools, that for the first time since I came on the Continent I was reminded of England. I meant, in real truth, that there was the same easy-going and absence of system on all sides, the same powerlessness and indifference of the State, the same independence in single institutions, the same free course for abuses, the same confusion, the same lack of all idea of *co-ordering* things, as the French say,—that is, of making them work fitly together to a fit end: the same waste of power, therefore, the same extravagance and the same poverty of result, of which the civil organisation of England offers so many instances. Modern States cannot either do without free institutions, or do without a rationally planned and effective civil organisation. Unlike in other things, Austria, Rome, and England are alike in this, that the civil organisation of each implies, at the present day, a denial or an ignorance of the right of mind and reason to rule human affairs. At Rome this right is sacrificed in the name of religion; in Austria, in the name of loyalty; in England, in the name of liberty. All respectable names; but none of them will in the long run save its invoker, if he persists in disregarding the inevitable laws which govern the life of modern society.

Every one is accustomed to hear that France paid the horrors of her great Revolution as the price for having a *tabula rasa* upon which to build a new civil organisation. But what one learns when one goes upon the Continent and looks a little closely into these things, is, that all the most progressive States of the Continent have followed the example of France, and have transformed or are transforming their civil organisation. Italy is transforming hers by virtue of the great opportunity which the events of the last fifteen years have given her. Prussia transformed hers from 1807 to 1812, by virtue of the stern lesson which her disasters and humiliation had then read her. Russia is at this moment accomplishing a transformation yet more momentous. The United States of America came into the world, it may be said, with a *tabula rasa* for a modern civil organisation to be built on, and they have never had any other. What I say is, that everywhere around us in the world, wherever there is life and progress, we find a civil organisation that is modern; and this is in States which have not, like France, gone through a tremendous revolution, as well as in France itself.

Who will deny that England has life and progress? but who will deny also that her course begins to show signs of uncertainty and embarrassment? This is because even an energy like hers cannot exempt her from the obligation of obeying natural laws; and yet she tries to exempt herself from it when she endeavours to meet the requirements of a modern time and of modern society with a civil organisation which is, from the top of it to the bottom, not modern. Transform it she must, unless she means to come at last to the same sentence as the Church of Sardis: "Thou hast a name that thou livest, and art dead." However, on no part of this immense task of transformation have I now to touch, except on that part which relates to education. But this part, indeed, is the most important of all; and it is the part whose happy accomplishment may render that of all the rest, instead of being troubled and difficult, gradual and easy.

About popular education I have here but a very few words to say. People are at last beginning to see in what condition this really is amongst us. Obligatory instruction is talked of. But what is the capital difficulty in the way of obligatory instruction, or indeed any national system of instruction, in this country? It is this: that the moment the working class of this country have this question of instruction really brought home to them, their self-respect will make them demand, like the working classes on the Continent, *public* schools, and not schools which the clergyman, or the squire, or the mill-owner, calls "my school." And what is the capital difficulty in the way of giving them public schools? It is this: that the public school for the people must rest upon the municipal organisation of the country. In France, Germany, Italy, Switzerland, the public elementary school has, and exists by having, the commune, and the municipal government of the commune, as its foundations, and it could not exist without them. But we in England have our municipal organisation still to get; the country districts, with us, have at present only the feudal and ecclesiastical organisation of the Middle Ages, or of France before the Revolution. This is what the people who talk so glibly about obligatory instruction, and the Conscience Clause, and our present abundant supply of schools, never think of. The real preliminary to an effective system of popular education is, in fact, to provide the country with an effective municipal organisation; and here, then, is at the outset an illustration of what I said, that modern societies need a civil organisation which is modern.[1]

[1] France had, in 1865, 37,500 communes, and nearly 37,500,000 inhabitants; about one commune, therefore, to every 1000 inhabitants. The mayor of the commune is named by the Crown, and represents the State, the central power; the municipal

We have nearly all of us reached the notion that popular education it is the State's duty to deal with. Secondary and superior instruction many of us still think should be left to take care of themselves. Well, this is what was generally thought, or at any rate practised, in old times, all over Europe. I have shown how the State's taking secondary instruction seriously in hand dates, in Prussia, from Wilhelm von Humboldt in 1809; in the same year, a year for Prussia of trouble and anxious looking forward, he created the University of Berlin. In Switzerland the State's effective dealing with all kinds of public instruction dates from within the last thirty years;

council, of which the mayor is president, is elected by universal suffrage of the commune.

We have in England 655 unions and about 12,000 parishes; but our communes, or municipal centres, ought at the French rate to be 20,000 in number. Nor is this number, perhaps, more than is required in order to supply a proper basis for the national organisation of our elementary schools. A municipal organisation being once given, the object should be to withdraw the existing elementary schools from their present private management, and to reconstitute them on a municipal basis. This is not the place to enter into details as to the manner in which such a withdrawal is to be effected; I will remark only that all reforms which stop short of such a withdrawal and reconstitution are and must be mere patchwork.

in Italy it dates from 1859. In all these countries the idea of a sound civil organisation of modern society has been found to involve the idea of an organisation of secondary and superior instruction by public authority, by the State.

The English reader will ask: What inconvenience has arisen in England from pursuing the old practice? The investigations of the Schools Enquiry Commission, I feel sure, will have made it clear that we have not a body of 65,000 boys of the middle and upper classes receiving so good an instruction as 65,000 boys of the same classes are receiving in the higher schools of Prussia, or even of France. The English reader will not refuse to believe, though no Royal Commission has yet made enquiries on this point, that we have not a body of 6300 university students in England receiving so good an instruction as the 6300 matriculated students in the Prussian universities, or even as the far more numerous students in the French faculties, are receiving. Neither is the secondary and superior instruction given in England on the whole so good, nor is it given, on the whole, in schools of so good a standing. Of course, what good instruction there is, and what schools of good standing there are to get it in, fall chiefly to the lot of the upper class. It is on the middle class that the inconvenience, such as it is, of getting indifferent instruction, or getting it in schools of indifferent standing, mainly comes. This inconvenience, as it strikes one after seeing attentively the schools of the Continent, has two aspects. It has a social aspect, and it has an intellectual aspect.

The social inconvenience is this. On the Continent, the upper and middle class are brought up on one and the same plane. In England the middle class, as a rule, *is brought up on the second plane.* One hears many discussions as to the limits between the middle and the upper class in England. From an educational point of view these limits are perfectly clear. Half-a-dozen famous schools, Oxford or Cambridge, the army or navy, and those posts in the public service supposed to be posts for gentlemen,—these are the schools all or any one of which give a training, a stamp, a cast of ideas, which make a sort of association of all those who share them, and this association is the upper class. Except by one of these modes of access an Englishman does not, unless by some special play of aptitude or of circumstances, become a vital part of this association, for he does not bring with him the cast of ideas in which its bond of union lies. This cast of ideas is naturally for the most part that of the most powerful and prominent part of the association, the aristocracy. The professions furnish the more numerous but the less prominent part; in no country, accordingly, do the professions so naturally and generally share the cast of ideas of the aristocracy as in England. This cast of ideas, judged from its good side, is characterised by a high spirit, by dignity, by a just sense of the greatness of great affairs,— all of them governing qualities; and the professions have accordingly long recruited the governing force of the aristocracy, and assisted it to rule. Judged from its bad side, this cast of ideas is characterised by its indisposition and incapacity for science, for systematic knowledge. The professions are on the Continent the stronghold of science and systematic knowledge; in England, from the reason above assigned, they are not.

They are also in England separate, to a degree unknown on the Continent, from the commercial and industrial class with which in social standing they are naturally on a level. So we have amongst us the spectacle of a middle class cut in two in a way unexampled anywhere else.; of a professional class brought up on the first plane, with fine and governing qualities, but without the idea of science; while that immense business-class, which is becoming so important a power in all countries, on which the future so much depends, and which in the leading schools of other countries fills so large a place, is in England brought up on the second plane, cut off from the aristocracy and the professions, and without governing qualities.

If only, in compensation, it had science, systematic knowledge! The stronghold of science should naturally be in a nation's middle class, who have neither luxury nor bodily toil to bar them from it. But here comes in the intellectual inconvenience of the bad condition of the mass of our secondary schools. On the Continent, if the professions were as aristocratic in their indifference to science as they are here, the business class, educated as it is, would at once wrest the lead from them, and would be fit to do so. But here in England, the business class is not only inferior to the professions in the social stamp of its places of training, it is actually inferior to them, maimed and incomplete as their intellectual development is, in its intellectual development. Short as the offspring of our public schools and universities come of the idea of science and systematic knowledge, the offspring of our middle class academies probably come, if that be possible, even shorter. What these academies fail to give in social and governing qualities, they do not make up for in intellectual power.

If this is true, then that our middle class does not yet itself see the defects of its own education, perceives no practical inconvenience to itself from them, and is satisfied with things as they are, is no reason for regarding this state of things without disquietude. "He that wandereth out of the way of understanding shall remain in the congregation of the dead;" sooner or later, in spite of his self-confidence, in spite of his energy, in spite of his capital, he must so remain, by virtue of nature's laws. But if the English business class can listen to testimonies that in the judgment of others, at any rate, its inferior education is beginning to threaten it with practical inconvenience, such testimonies are formidably plentiful. A diplomatist of great experience, not an Englishman but much attached to England, who in the course of the acquisition and the construction of the Italian lines of railroad, had been brought much in contact with young men of business of all nations, told me that the young Englishman of this class was manifestly inferior, both in manners and instruction, to the corresponding young men of other countries. That is, he had been brought up, as I say, on a lower plane. And the Swiss and Germans aver, if you question them as to the benefit they have got from their *Realschulen* and Polytechnicums, that in every part of the world their men of business trained in those schools are beating the English when they meet on equal terms as to capital; and that when English capital, as so often happens, is superior, the advantage of the Swiss or the German in instruction tends more and more to balance this superiority. M. Duruy, till lately the French Minister of Public Instruction, confirms this averment, not as against England in especial, but generally, by saying that all over the Continent the young North German, or the young Swiss of Zurich or Basle, is seizing, by reason of his better instruction, a confidence and a command in business which the young men of no other nation can dispute with him. This confidence, whether as yet completely justified or not by success, is a force which will go far to ensure its own triumph.

But the idea of science and systematic knowledge is wanting to our whole instruction alike, and not only to that of our business class. While this idea is getting more and more power upon the Continent, and while its application there is leading to more and considerable results, we in England, having done marvels by the rule of thumb, are still inclined to disbelieve in the paramount importance, in whatever department, of any other. And yet in Germany every one will tell you that the explanation of the late astonishing achievements of Prussia is simply that every one concerned in them had thoroughly learnt his business on the

o

best plan by which it was possible to teach it to him. In nothing do England and the Continent at the present moment more strikingly differ than in the prominence which is now given to the idea of science there, and the neglect in which this idea still lies here; a neglect so great that we hardly even know the use of the word science in its strict sense, and only employ it in a secondary and incorrect sense. The English notion,— for which there is much to be said if it were not pushed to such an excess,—is, that you come to do a thing right by doing it, and not by first learning how to do it right and then doing it. The French, who in the extent and solidity of their instruction are, as a nation, so much behind the Germans, are yet in their idea of science quite in a line with the Germans, and ahead of us. That is because there is in France a considerable highly instructed class into whose whole training this idea of science has come, and whose whole influence goes to procure its application. We have no considerable class of this kind. We have, probably, a larger reading class than the French, but reading for amusement, not study; occupied with books of popular reading that leave the mind as inaccurate, as shallow, and as unscientific as it was before. The French have a much more considerable class than we have which really studies. A good test of this is the description of foreign books which get translated. Now the English reader will, perhaps, be surprised to hear that a German scientific book of any sort,—on philosophy, history, art, religion, etc.,—is much more sure of being translated into French than it is into English. A popular story or a popular religious book is sure enough of being translated into English; there is a public for a translation of that; but in France there is a public, not large certainly, but large enough to take an edition or two, for a translation of works not of this popular character.[1] In Germany, of course, there is a yet far larger public of such a kind. The very matter of public instruction suggests an illustration on this point, and an illustration at my own expense. It has been

[1] There is nothing like an illustration, so let me name these three standard works, Creuzer's "Symbolik," Preller's "Römische Mythologie," and Von Hammer's "Geschichte des Osmanischen Reichs," of each of which there is a translation in French, and none in English.

quite the order of the day here, for some years past, to discuss the subject of popular education. This is a subject which can no more be known without being treated comparatively, than anatomy can be known without being treated comparatively. When it was under discussion in foreign countries, these countries procured accounts of what was done for popular education elsewhere, which were published, found a public to study them for their bearing on the general question, and went through two or three editions. But I doubt whether two hundred people in this country have read Mr. Pattison's report, or mine, on the popular schools of the Continent; simply because the notion of treating a matter of this kind as a matter of scientific study hardly occurs to any one in this country; but almost every one treats it as a matter which he can settle by the light of his own personal experience, and of what he calls his practical good sense.

Our rule of thumb has cost us dear already, and is probably destined to cost us dearer still. It is only by putting an unfair and extravagant strain on the wealth and energy of the country, that we have managed to hide from ourselves the inconvenience we suffer, even in the lines where we think ourselves most successful, from our want of systematic instruction and science. I was lately saying to one of the first mathematicians in England, who has been a distinguished senior wrangler at Cambridge and a practical mechanician besides, that in one department at any rate,—that of mechanics and engineering,—we seemed, in spite of the absence of special schools, good instruction, and the idea of science, to get on wonderfully well. "On the contrary," said he, "we get on wonderfully ill. Our engineers have no real scientific instruction, and we let them learn their business at our expense by the rule of thumb; but it is a ruinous system of blunder and plunder. A man without the requisite scientific knowledge undertakes to build a difficult bridge; he builds three which tumble down, and so learns how to build a fourth which stands; but somebody pays for the three failures. In France or Switzerland he would not have been suffered to build his first bridge until he had satisfied competent persons that he knew how to build it, because abroad they cannot afford our extravagance. The scientific training of the foreign engineers is therefore perfectly right. Take the present cost per mile of the construction of an English railway, and the cost per mile as it was twenty years ago ; and the comparison will give you a correct notion of what rule-of-thumb engineering, without special schools and without scientific instruction, has cost the country."

Our dislike of authority and our disbelief in science have combined to make us leave our school system, like so many other branches of our civil organisation, to take care of itself as it best could. Under such auspices, our school system has very naturally fallen all into confusion ; and though properly an intellectual agency, it has done and does nothing to counteract the indisposition to science which is our great intellectual fault. The result is, that we have to meet the calls of a modern epoch, in which the action of the working and middle class assumes a preponderating importance, and science tells in human affairs more and more, with a working class not educated at all, a middle class educated on the second plane, and the idea of science absent from the whole course and design of our education.

On popular education I have already touched so far as is proper for my present purpose. Secondary, and superior instruction remain. It is through secondary instruction that the social inconvenience I spoke of is to be remedied. The intellectual inconvenience is to be remedied through superior instruction, at first acting by itself, and then, through the teachers whom it forms and its general influence on society, acting on the secondary schools. I will sketch, guided by the comparative study of education which I have been enabled to make, the organisation of schools which seems to me required for this purpose. My part is simply to say what organisation seems to me to be required; it is for others to judge what organisation seems to them possible, or advisable to be attempted. The times, however, are moving; and what is not advisable to-day, may perhaps be called for to-morrow.

But the English reader will hardly, I think, have accompanied me thus far, without sharing the conclusion that at any rate a public system of schools is indispensable in modern communities

From the moment you seriously desire to have your schools efficient, the question between public and private schools is settled. Of public schools you can take guarantees, of private schools you cannot. Guarantees cannot be absolutely certain. It is possible for a private school, which has given no guarantees, to be good ; it is possible for a public school, which has given guarantees, to be bad. But even in England the disbelief in human reason is hardly strong enough to make us seriously contend that a rational being cannot frame for a known purpose guarantees which give him, at any rate, more numerous chances of reaching that purpose than he would have without them.

If public schools are a necessity, then an Education Minister is a necessity. Merely for administrative convenience he is, indeed, indispensable. But what is yet more important than administrative convenience is to have what an Education Minister alone supplies, *a centre in which to fix responsibility*.[1]

[1] I need hardly point out that at present, with our Lord President, Vice-President, and Committee of Council on Education, we entirely fail to get, for primary instruction, this distinct centre of responsibility.

The country at large is not yet educated enough, political considerations too much overbear all others, for a minister with a board of six or seven councillors, like the minister at Berlin, to be left alone to perform such a task as the reconstruction of public education in this country must at first be. A High Council of Education, such as exists in France and Italy, comprising without regard to politics the personages most proper to be heard on questions of public education, a consultative body only, but whose opinion the minister should be obliged to take on all important measures not purely administrative, would be an invaluable aid to an English Education Minister, an invaluable institution in our too political country.

One or two matters which I have already approached or touched in the course of this volume are matters on which it would be the natural function of such a Council to advise. It would be its function to advise on the propriety of subjecting children under a certain age to competitive examination, in order to determine their admission to public foundations. It would be its function to advise on the employment of the examination test for the public service; whether this security should, as at present, be relied on exclusively, or whether it should not be preceded by securities for the applicant having previously passed a certain time under training and teachers of a certain character, and stood certain examinations in connection with that training. It would be its function to advise on the organisation of school and university examinations, and their adjustment to one another. It would be its function to advise on the graduation of schools in proper stages, from the elementary to the highest school; it would be its function to advise on school books, and, above all, on studies, and on the plan of work for schools; a business which, as I have said, is more and more inviting discussion and ripening for settlement. We have excellent materials in England for such a Council. Properly composed, and properly representing the grave interests concerned in the questions it has to treat, it would not only have great weight with the minister, but great weight, as an illustrious, unpaid, deliberative, and non-ministerial body, with the country, and would greatly strengthen the minister's hand for important reforms.

Provincial School Boards, too, we have in this country very good materials for forming, and this institution of Germany is well suited to our habits, supplies a basis for local action, and preserves one from the inconveniences of an over-centralised system like that of France. Eight or ten Provincial School Boards should be formed, not too large, five or six members being the outside number for each Board, and one member being paid. This board would be administrative; it would represent the State in the country, keeping the Education Minister informed of local requirements and of the state of schools in each district; being the direct public organ of communication with the schools, superintending the execution of all public regulations applied to them, visiting them so far as may be necessary, and representing the State by the presence of one of its members at their main annual examinations. An elaborate system of inspection, modelled on that of primary schools, is out of place when applied to higher schools; the French school authorities complained to me that they were over-inspected, and no doubt there are evident and solid objections to putting a *lycée* on the same footing, as regards inspection, with an elementary school. The Prussian system is far better, which resolves inspection, for higher schools, mainly into a concert of the State with the school authorities in great examinations,—as effective a way of inspection, in real truth, as can be found. What special visits may happen to be required are best made, as in Prussia, by members of the Provincial Boards, or by councillors of the Central Department; and a staff of school inspectors for higher schools is neither requisite nor desirable.

Where are the English higher schools, it will be asked, with which this Minister, this Council, and these School Boards are to deal? Guided by the experience of every country I have visited, I will venture to lay down certain propositions which may help to supply an answer to this question. Wherever there is a school-endowment, there is a right of public supervision, and, if necessary, of a re-settlement of the endowment by public authority. Wherever, again, there is a school-endowment from the Crown or the State, there is a right to the State of participation in the management of the endowment, and of representation on the body which manages it. These two propositions, which in ten years' time will even in England be admitted on all hands to be indisputable, supply all that is necessary for a public system of education. School endowments will certainly be dealt with ere long, and the extraordinary immunity which, from the peculiar habits and isolation of this country, the corporations or private trustees administering them have hitherto enjoyed, is really a reason for applying the principles of common sense and public policy, when they are at last applied to these matters, the more stringently instead of the less stringently. Endowments enough have merited an absolute withdrawal from their present bad application, and an absolute appropriation by public authority for the purposes of a better application, to furnish the State with means for creating, as a commencement, a certain number of Royal or Public schools, to be under the direct control of the Education Department and the Provincial Boards; and in which all the regulations for management, fees, books, studies, methods, and examinations, devised by public authority as most expedient, should have force unreservedly. Other schools would be found offering to place themselves under public administration, as soon as this administration began to inspire respect and confidence; and organised rightly, it would immediately inspire respect and confidence. A body of truly public schools would thus be formed, offering to the middle classes places of instruction with sound securities and with an honourable standing. Nor would these new schools long be in antagonism with our present chief schools, and following a different line of movement from them. Some of our present chief schools, like Eton and Westminster and Christ's Hospital, are royal foundations. Here the right of the State to have a share in the whole administration of the institution, and a voice in the nomination of the masters, immediately arises. Others, like Winchester, Rugby, and Harrow, are not royal foundations, but all of them are foundation schools, and therefore to all of them, as such, a right of public supervision applies. The best form this supervision can possibly take is that of a participation, as in Germany, by the public authority represented through the Provincial School Boards or through members of the High Council of Education, in their main examinations. On these examinations matriculation at the university,[1] and access to all the higher lines of public employment should be made to depend. The pupils of private schools should be admitted to undergo them. In this way every endowed school in the kingdom would have yearly an all-important examination following a line traced or sanctioned by the most competent authority, the Superior Council of Education; and with a direct or indirect representation of this authority taking part in it. The organisation of studies in our very best schools could not fail to gain by this; in all but the very best, it would be its regeneration. Even in England, where the general opinion would be opposed to requiring, as in Germany, for the appointment of all public schoolmasters the sanction of a public

---

[1] But there should be a different matriculation examination for each faculty, and, except for the faculties of theology and arts, Greek should not be required.

authority, there could be no respectable objections urged to such a mode of public intervention as this; the one bulwark, to repeat Wilhelm von Humboldt's words, which we can set up against the misuse of their patronage by private trustees. And we should at the same time get the happiest check put to the cram and bad teaching of private schools, by compelling them either to adjust their studies to sound and serious examinations, or to cease to impose upon the credulity of ignorant parents.

The mention of the matriculation examination brings me to superior or university instruction. This is, in the opinion of the best judges, the weakest part of our whole educational system, and we must not hope to improve effectually the secondary school without doing something for the schools above it, with which it has an intimate natural connection. The want of the idea of science, of systematic knowledge, is, as I have said again and again, the capital want, at this moment, of English education and of English life; it is the university, or the superior school, which ought to foster this idea. The university or the superior school ought to provide facilities, after the general education is finished, for the young man to go on in the line where his special aptitudes lead him, be it that of languages and literature, of mathematics, of the natural sciences, of the application of these sciences, or any other line, and follow the studies of this line systematically under first-rate teaching. Our great universities, Oxford and Cambridge, do next to nothing towards this end. They are, as Signor Matteucci called them, *hauts lycées;* and though invaluable in their way as places where the youth of the upper class prolong to a very great age, and under some very admirable influences, their school education, and though in this respect to be envied by the youth of the upper class abroad and if possible instituted for their benefit, yet, with their college and tutor system, nay, with their examination and degree system, they are still, in fact, *schools*, and do not carry education beyond the stage of general and school education. The examination for the degree of bachelor of arts, which we place at the end of our three years' university course, is merely the *Abiturientenexamen* of Germany, the *épreuve du baccalauréat* of France, placed in both of these countries at the entrance to university studies instead of, as with us, at their close. Scientific instruction, university instruction, really begins when the degree of bachelor (*bas chevalier*, knight of low degree) is taken, and the preparation for mastership in any line of study, or for doctorship (fitness to teach it), commences. But for mastership or doctorship, Oxford and Cambridge have, as is well known, either no examination at all, or an examination which is a mere form; they have consequently no instruction directed to these grades; no real university-instruction, therefore, at all. A machinery for such instruction they have, indeed, in their possession; but it is notorious that they do not practically use it.

The University of London labours under a yet graver defect as an organ of scientific or superior instruction. It is a mere *collegium*, or board, of examiners. It gives no instruction at all, but it examines in the different lines of study, and gives degrees in them. It has real university-examinations, which Oxford and Cambridge have not; and these examinations are conducted by an independent board, and not by college tutors. This is excellent; but nevertheless it falls immensely short of what is needed. The idea of a university is, as I have already said, that of an institution not only offering to young men facilities for graduating in that line of study to which their aptitudes direct them, but offering to them, also, *facilities for following that line of study systematically, under first-rate instruction.* This second function is of incalculable importance; of far greater importance, even, than the first. It is impossible to overvalue the importance to a young man of being brought in contact with a first-rate teacher of his matter of study, and of getting from him a clear notion of what the systematic study of it means. Such instruction is so far from being yet organised in this country, that it even requires a gifted student to feel the want of it; and such a student must go to Paris, or Heidelberg, or Berlin, because England cannot give him what he wants. Some do go; an admirable English mathematician who did not, told me that he should never recover the loss of the two years which after his degree he wasted without fit instruction at an English university, when he ought to have been under superior instruction, for which the present university course in England makes no provision. I daresay he *will* recover it, for a man of genius counts no worthy effort too hard; but who can estimate the loss to the mental training and intellectual habits of the country, from an absence,—so complete that it needs genius to be sensible of it, and costs genius an effort to repair it,—of all regular public provision for the scientific study and teaching of any branch of knowledge?

England had, in 1865, twenty millions of inhabitants, and the matriculated students in England numbered then about 3500. Prussia, — the Prussia of this volume, — has 18,500,000 inhabitants, and 6362 matriculated students. France has at least as large a proportion of her population coming under superior instruction. England, with her wealth and importance, has barely one-half the proportion of her population coming, even nominally, under superior instruction, that Prussia and France have. But this comparison by no means gives the full measure of her disadvantage, because, as I have just shown, Oxford and Cambridge being in reality but *hauts lycées*, and London University being only a board of examiners, the very majority of even the 3500 students of superior instruction whom England nominally possesses, do not, in fact, come under superior instruction at all. This entire absence of the crowning of the edifice not only tends to give us, as I have said, a want of scientific intellect in all departments, but it tends to weaken and obliterate, in the whole nation, the sense of the value and importance of human knowledge; to vulgarise us, to exaggerate our estimate, naturally excessive, of the importance of material advantages, and to make our teachers, all but the very best of them, pursue their calling in a mere trade spirit, and with an eye to little except these advantages.

Exactly the same effect which in the field of university teaching our want of any real course of superior instruction produces, is produced, in the field of the applied sciences, by our want of special schools like the School of Arts and Trades in Paris, or the *Gewerbe-Institut* of Berlin, or the Zurich Polytechnicum. It is the same crowning of the edifice of instruction which is wanting in both cases; the same bad intellectual habits and defective intellectual action, which are in both cases fostered by this want. Our Science and Art Department at South Kensington is a recent experiment in this country, and has been a mark for much obloquy here. I am totally unconnected with that department; I am barely acquainted with Mr. Cole who directs it, and I have not the special knowledge requisite for criticising its operations. But I am bound to say that everywhere on the Continent I found a strong interest directed to this department, a strong sense of its importance and of the excellent effect it had already produced on our industry, with a conviction that in the mere interests of this industry we should be obliged to go on and give to this idea of a special school greater development. I, too, believe that we must have a system of special schools; but this is a subject which well deserves a separate study, and some one to treat it who is better qualified for the business than I am. I touch on it here merely as a branch of the great subject of superior instruction,—the instruction which is properly, and in all but special cases, to be given by universities.

To extend this amongst us is the great matter. Considering the wealth and occupations of the middle and upper classes of this country, we ought to have at least 8000 students coming under this instruction. The Education Department, by the leaving examination which I have mentioned,—an examination to be held at the different schools and to represent the present matriculation examination, —should take the admission of university students entirely out of the hands of the colleges, and thus save Oxford and Cambridge from the absolute *non-valeurs* (to use M. Duruy's term) of which at present, owing to the laches of many of the colleges, they have far too many. The degree examination should be taken out of the hands of the college tutors, and entrusted, for reasons which I will give presently, to a board of examiners named by public authority. Beyond these changes, it is not in Oxford and Cambridge that the great work to be done is to be accomplished. All around me I hear people talking of university reform, university extension; all these projects end in

Oxford or Cambridge, and the most liberal of them with a year's residence there. If there is one thing which my foreign experience has left me convinced of,—as convinced of as I am of our actual want of superior instruction,—it is this: that we must take this instruction to the students, and not hope to bring the students to the instruction. We must get out of our heads all notion of making the mass of students come and reside three years, or two years, or one year, or even one month, at Oxford or Cambridge, which neither suit their circumstances nor offer them the instruction they want. We must plant faculties in the eight or ten principal seats of population, and let the students follow lectures there from their own homes, or with whatever arrangements for their living they and their parents choose. It would be everything for the great seats of population to be thus made intellectual centres as well as mere places of business; for the want of this, at present, Liverpool and Leeds are mere overgrown provincial towns, while Strasburg and Lyons are European cities. Oxford and Cambridge would contribute in the noblest and most useful way to the spread of university instruction, if they placed a number of their professors,— of whom they themselves make little use owing to the college system,—in these new faculties, to be established in London or the provinces, where they might render incalculable service, and, still retaining the title of Oxford or Cambridge professors, unite things, new and old, and help in the happiest manner to inaugurate a truly national system of superior instruction. Oxford and Cambridge can, from the nature of things, be nowadays important schools only in theology, arts, and the mathematical and natural sciences. Owing to their college system, which for certain purposes, as I have said, and for a certain class, works well, they do not really need half their professors in even these three faculties, and could spare half of them for use elsewhere. They are actually bad places for schools in law and medicine, and all their professors in these faculties they might with advantage employ where there would be a better field for their services. All future application of Oxford and Cambridge emoluments to national purposes might, with advantage to the country, and honour to Oxford and

Cambridge themselves, be made in this direction of endowing chairs for professors and exhibitions for students in university faculties to be organised in the great towns of England. The university of London should be re-cast and should have faculties formed in connection with it, in order to give some public voice and place to superior instruction in the richest capital of the world; and for this purpose the strangely devised and anomalous organisations of King's College and University College should be turned to account, and *co-ordered*, as the French say, with the University of London. Contributions from Oxford and Cambridge, and new appointments, might supply what was wanting to fill the faculties, which in London, the capital of the country, should, as at Paris or Berlin, be very strong. London would then really have, what it has not at present, a university.

It is with our superior instruction as with so much else; we have plenty of scattered materials, but these materials need to be co-ordered, and made, instead of being useless or getting in one another's way as at present, to work harmoniously to one great design. This design should be, to form centres of superior instruction in at least ten different parts of England, with first-rate professors to give this instruction. These professors should of course be grouped in faculties, each faculty having its dean. So entirely have Oxford and Cambridge become mere *hauts lycées*, so entirely has the very idea of a real university been lost by them, that the professors there are not even organised in faculties; and their action is on this account alone, if it were not on other accounts also, perfectly feeble and incoherent. The action of professors grouped in faculties, and concerting, as the professors and *Privatdocenten* of a faculty concert in Germany, their instruction together, is quite another thing. In a place like London all the five faculties of arts, mathematical and natural sciences, theology, law, and medicine, should of course be represented; but it is by no means necessary that each centre of superior instruction should have all these five faculties. Durham, for instance, ought probably to have, as I think a Royal Commission once proposed, but two faculties,—a faculty of theology, and a faculty of mathematical and natural sciences. The requirements of different localities, and the facilities they offer for certain lines, must be taken into account. It is evident, for example, that faculties of medicine are best placed in very large towns, where hospitals and hospital patients are numerous.

Neither is it by any means necessary, or even expedient, that each centre of faculties should have the power of conferring degrees. To maintain a uniform standard of examination and a uniform value for degrees is most important, and this is impossible when there are too many bodies examining for degrees and giving them. Germany suffers from having too many universities granting degrees, and from these degrees bearing a very unequal value. We have two old and important universities, Oxford and Cambridge ; one new and important university, London, and we want no more degree-granting bodies than these. The different centres of faculties throughout the country should be in connection with one or other of the universities, according as they may have received professors from them, or may be nearest to one or the other of them; and each of these three universities should have its board of examiners, composed of professors holding chairs in its district, and with the Superior Council of Education represented on each board. Thus composing your examining board substantially of professors, you would avoid the objection urged against the present examinations of the London University, that they are *in the air*, and that their standard fluctuates: composing it from among the professors of a third part of England, you would avoid the inconveniences of letting the teachers of any set of students have the sole decision of the degrees to be granted to them. All the lesser examinations, such as should at the end of each year be held in order to determine whether the student makes progress and is to be allowed to go on with his course, belong naturally, in each centre, to the professors in that centre.

Such a system as that of which I have thus given the bare outline, can be properly organised only by an Education Minister, with the concert and advice of a Superior Council of Public Instruction, and, if necessary, with the help of a public grant. 'The intervention of the State becomes especially necessary in superior instruction, because here the body of public opinion educated enough to discern what is wanted gets smaller than ever, while the importance of organising your instruction well and committing it to first-rate men becomes greater than ever. It is not from any love of bureaucracy that men like Wilhelm von Humboldt, ardent friends of human dignity and liberty, have had recourse to a department of State in organising universities; it is because an Education Minister supplies you, for the discharge of certain critical functions, the agent who will perform them in the greatest blaze of daylight and with the keenest sense of responsibility. Convocation made me formerly a professor, and I am very grateful to Convocation; but Convocation is not a fit body to have the appointment of professors. It is far too numerous, and the sense of responsibility does not tell upon it strongly enough. A board is not a fit body to have the appointment of professors; men will connive at a job as members of a board who single-handed would never have perpetrated it. Even the Crown,— that is, the Prime Minister,—is not the fit power to have the appointment of professors; for the Prime Minister is above all a political functionary, and feels political influences overwhelmingly. An Education Minister, directly representing all the interests of learning and intelligence in this great country, a full mark for their criticism and conscious of his responsibility to them, *that* is the power to whom to give the appointment of professors, not for his own sake, but for the sake of public education. Even if the appointment of professors at Oxford and Cambridge be left as at present, the appointment of every professor in the new faculties should be vested in the Education Minister, and he should be responsible for it; though the faculties should have the right, as they have abroad, of themselves proposing to him candidates they may think proper.

Putting Oxford and Cambridge out of the question, all other places in England, even London, would have so much to gain by a regular public organisation being given to superior instruction in them, and by their professors acquiring the status and authority of public functionaries, that I cannot doubt that bodies like the Senate of the London University, the Council of London University

College, or the trustees of Owens College, at Manchester, would gladly co-operate with an Education Minister in transforming and co-ordering their institutions so as to give them a national character and an increased effectiveness. Several of the personages in the Senate of the London University are personages who would naturally have a place in any Superior Council of Public Instruction. Following the Prussian division of school interests into *externa* and *interna*, trustees might remain charged with *externa*, the management of property; while *interna*, the appointment of professors and the organisation of faculties, devolved upon the Education department. The great towns chosen to be the seats of the new faculties would most of them gladly charge themselves with providing a fit habitation for a public establishment adding so much to their resources and importance. Many of them would furnish an annual contribution to the expenses of the faculties. I believe there would be more chance of a brisk competition among the chief towns for the honour of being made seats of university faculties, than of their undervaluing it. At any rate, no such town would be the seat of them long without learning to value them. The important thing is to establish them.

Once established, they should be employed as in a country which, relying on its good intentions, its industry, and its wealth, has too long set at nought Solomon's warning: "*They that hate instruction love death.*" The end to have in view is, that every one who presents himself to exercise any calling shall have received for a certain length of time the best instruction preliminary to that calling. This is not, it must be repeated again and again, an absolute security for his exercising the calling well, but it is the best security. It is a thousand times better security than the mere examination-test on which with such ignorant confidence we are now, in cases where we take any security at all, leaning with our whole weight. The Civil Service Examination should be used in strict subordination to this better and ampler security, and with a view of keeping it real. For some classes of post in the public service the having passed the leaving examination of a public school ought to be demanded: for others, the having gone through the appointed courses and passed the appointed examinations in certain faculties or in certain special schools ; for all, one or the other. Then, and not till then, may come in, as a confirmatory and supplementary test, a rationally regulated civil service examination. No minister of religion, to whom, as such, any public functions are assigned, no magistrate, no schoolmaster of a higher school, no lawyer, no doctor, should be allowed to exercise his function without having come for a certain time under superior instruction and passed its examinations. The Pharmaceutical Society should be co-ordered with the faculties of medicine, and no druggist should be allowed to practise without its instruction and certificates. It is with the industrial class that the great difficulty of applying superior instruction arises; this class so large, wealthy, and important, and which needs superior instruction so much just because it feels that it needs it so little. Owens College at Manchester with its 100 students, and London University with its 450 students (even if these, who have no appointed faculty instruction, are to be called university students at all), sufficiently show, what is well known, that practically the English industrial class cannot be said to come under superior instruction at all. Their present indifference to it, however, affords no true criterion for judging of their probable willingness to accept it if it were properly organised, brought home to their doors, and made compatible with the necessary conditions of their lives.

Thus I have attempted to sketch in outline the plan of reorganisation for English instruction which is suggested almost irresistibly by a study of public instruction in other European countries, and of the actual condition and prospects of the modern world. The reorganisation proposed will to many people in England appear chimerical. Yet I have a profound conviction that if our country is destined, as I trust it is destined, still to live and prosper, the next quarter of a century will see a reconstruction of English education as entire as that which I have recommended in these remarks, however impossible such a reconstruction may to many now seem.

APPENDIX.

LIST of the COURSES of LECTURES by Professors, *Privatdocenten*, and Readers, in the University of Berlin, during the Winter *Semester* of 1865-66.

I. FACULTY OF THEOLOGY.

Full Professors.

1. Special Dogmatics (6 hours a week).
2. Theology of the New Testament, and Life of Christ (5 hours).
3. God's Kingdom till the Coming of Christ (1 h.)
4. Introduction to the books of the Old Testament (5 h.)
5. Explanation of the Psalms (5 h.)
6. Life of Christ, and Critical History of the Gospels (2 h.)
7. History of the Church of the Reformation (6 h.)
8. Exercises in Catechisation and Preaching (2 h.)
9. The same (2 h.)
10. Practical Theology (5 h.)

11. The Creeds (1 h.)
12. Symbolical Theology, and Introduction to the Criticism of the New Testament (5 h.)

Assistant Professors.

13. The book of Judges (1 h.)
14. The book of Genesis (5 h.)
15. Life and Doctrine of St. Paul (1 h.)
16. The Epistle to the Romans (5 h.)
17. The Circle of Knowledge and Methodology (2 h.)
18. Church History, part 1 (5 h.)
19. Archæology and Patristic Study (1 h.)
20. Homiletics, theoretical and practical (2 h.)
21. Biblical History (4 h.)
22. Dogmatics (1 h.)
23. The book of Isaiah (6 h.)
24. Introduction of the books of the Old Testament (5 h.)

Privatdocenten.

25. The book of Genesis (5 h.)
26. Prophetical Inspiration (2 h.)
27. The book of Isaiah (5 h.)
28. History of the Israelitish Worship (2 h.)
29. The book of Isaiah (5 h.)
30. Chaldaic and Syriac Grammar (2 h.)
31. Three of St. Paul's Epistles explained (2 h.)
32. History of the Christian Dogmas (5 h.)
33. Symbolical Theology (1 h.)

APPENDIX. 231

34. The Dogmatical passages in the Old and New Testament explained (5 h.)
35. Church History, part 1 (5 h.)
36. History of the Christian Dogmas (5 h.)

II. FACULTY OF LAW.

Full Professors.

1. Psychology of Crimes (1 h.)
2. Natural Law, Philosophy of Law (4 h.)
3. Criminal Law (4 h.)
4. Criminal Procedure (2 h.)
5. Law of Nations (2 h.)
6. Private German Law, Commercial Law (5 h.)
7. Practical Exercises (1 h.)
8. The Pandects (1 h.)
9. Practical Law of the Pandects (6 h.)
10. History of English Law (1 h.)
11. Roman Law of Inheritance (2 h.)
12. Common and Prussian Civil Process (4 h.)
13. German and Prussian Public Law (4 h.)
14. Canon Law (4 h.)
15. Prussian Law (1 h.)
16. Methodology of Law (3 h.)
17. Prussian Civil Law (4 h.)
18. History of the German Empire and German Law (4 h.)
19. History of the Provincial Estates in Germany (3 h.)

20. The fourth book of Gaius explained (2 h.)
21. History of Roman Law (5 h.)
22. Institutes and Antiquities of Roman Law (5 h.)

Assistant Professors.

23. History and actual state of the German Confederation (3 h.)
24. Common Law of Prussia (4 h.)
25. French Civil Law (4 h.)
26. Catholic and Protestant Law of Marriage (1 h.)
27. Prussian Civil Law (4 h.)
28. Catholic and Protestant Canon Law (4 h.)
29. Ecclesiastical and Canon Law (4 h.)
30. Practice of Ecclesiastical and Canon Law (1 h.)
31. Capital Punishment (1 h.)
32. Common and Prussian Criminal Law (4 h.)
33. French Criminal Procedure (2 h.)
34. German Public Law, Rights of Sovereigns (2 h.)
35. Law of Nations (3 h.)
36. Practical Exercises on the Criminal Law (1 h.)

Privatdocenten.

37. Prussian Law (1 h.)
38. History of Roman Law (1 h.)
39. Institutes and Antiquities of Roman Law (4 h.)
40. Prussian Civil Law (4 h.)
41. Feudal Law (1 h.)
42. Private German Law (4 h.)

APPENDIX. 233

43. Commercial Law, Maritime Law, and Law of Exchange (4 h.)
44. History of Roman Law in Germany (1 h.)
45. History of the Empire, and of German Law (4 h.)
46. Prussian Law of Succession (1 h.)
47. Practical Exercises on the Jurisprudence of the Pandects (1 h.)
48. Institutes and Antiquities of Roman Law (5 h.)
49. Relations between Church and State (1 h.)
50. Ecclesiastical and Marriage Law (4 h.)
51. German Public Law, Private Rights of Sovereigns (2 h.)
52. Prussian Public Law (3 h.)
53. Practical Exercises on Public and Canon Law (1 h.)
54. Private Justice among the Romans (2 h.)
55. Roman Law of Succession (3 h.)
56. Modern Law of Exchange in Germany (1 h.)
57. Private Law and Feudal Law in Germany (4 h.)
58. Commercial and Maritime Law in Germany (4 h.)
59. The *Speculum Saxonicum* explained (2 h.)
60. History of the Empire, and of German Law (4 h.)
61. Interpretation of the Solutions in the Digests (1 h.)
62. Methodology of Law (3 h.)

III. FACULTY OF MEDICINE.

Full Professors.

1. On certain Discoveries of the Naturalists (1 h.)
2. Experimental Physiology (5 h.)

3. Practical Exercises in Experimental Physiology (1 h.)
4. Comparative Physiology with the Microscope (1 h.)
5. General History of Medicine (1 h.)
6. Pathology and Therapeutics (3 h.)
7. Clinical Medicine (6 h.)
8. Diseases of the Nervous System (5 h.) [1]
9. Medical Practice (6 h.)
10. History of Popular Maladies (1 h.)
11. General History of Medicine (3 h.)
12. Pathology and Therapeutics (5 h.)
13. Hernia (2 h.)
14. General and Special Surgery (4 h.)
15. Clinical Surgery and Clinical Ophthalmics, Clinical Surgery (5 h.) [1]
16. Experiments in Surgery and Anatomy.
17. Clinical Surgery and Clinical Ophthalmics (6 h.) [1]
18. Midwifery (4 h.)
19. Clinical Midwifery (6 h.) [1]
20. Practical Exercises in Midwifery (1 h.)
21. Excitant Drugs in Medicine (2 h.)
22. *Materia Medica* (6 h.)
23. Osteology (1 h.)
24. Anatomy of the Brain and Spinal Marrow (1 h.)
25. General Anatomy (6 h.)
26. Structure of the Human body, with the Microscope (1 h.)

[1] Delivered either at one of the hospitals, or at one of the medical institutions, of Berlin.

APPENDIX. 235

27. Practical Exercises in Anatomy (24 h.)
28. Methodology of Medicine (2 h.)
29. General Pathology and Therapeutics, and their History (4 h.)
30. *Materia Medica*, with Experiments (6 h.)
31. Pathological Anatomy (4 h.)
32. Practical Course of Anatomy and Pathology, with the Microscope (6 h.)
33. Practical Course of Pathological Osteology (6 h.)

Assistant Professors.

34. Spectacles (1 h.)
35. Ophthalmology (2 h.)
36. The same (2 h.)
37. Clinical Ophthalmics (6 h.)
38. Practical Course of Ophthalmics, with Experiments (1 h.)
39. General Surgery (6 h.)
40. Surgical Operations on Dead Bodies.
41. Diseases of Children (6 h.)
42. Errors of Modern Medicine (1 h.)
43. Hygiene (1 h.)
44. Theory and Practice of Treatment of Diseases of the Eye (4 h.)
45. Anatomy of the Organs of Sense (1 h.)
46. Osteology and Syndesmology of the Human Body (3 h.)
47. Public Hygiene (1 h.)
48. Legal Medicine (3 h.)

49. Medico-legal Dissection (6 h.)
50. The Nerves (2 h.)
51. Clinical Study of Diseases of the Nerves (6 h.)
52. Toxicology (2 h.)
53. Legal Medicine (3 h.)
54. Medico-legal Dissection (6 h.)
55. Pathology and Therapeutics (1 h.)
56. Auscultation (4 h.)
57. Clinical Lectures on Auscultation and Percussion (6 h.)[1]
58. Wounds (1 h.)
59. Fractures and Dislocations (2 h.)
60. Application of Bandages (3 h.)

Privatdocenten.

61. Diseases of the Teeth and Mouth (2 h.)
62. Diseases of the Teeth and their Cure, with Experiments (6 h.)
63. Surgical and Ophthalmological Experiments.
64. Drawing up of Prescriptions (2 h.)
65. Special Pathology and Therapeutics (6 h.)
66. Venereal Diseases (2 h.)
67. Cutaneous Diseases (2 h.)
68. Clinical Lectures on Diseases of Children (2 h.)
69. Diseases of the Ear (1 h.)
70. Moral Responsibility (1 h.)
71. Pathology of Venereal Diseases (1 h.)

[1] Delivered either at one of the hospitals, or at one of the medical institutions, of Berlin.

72. Surgery (6 h.)
73. Legal Medicine (2 h.)
74. Diseases of Women (2 h.)
75. Theory and Practice of Midwifery (4 h.)
76. Baths and Thermal Waters (2 h.)
77. Drawing up of Prescriptions (3 h.)
78. Physiological Effects of Gases (3 h.)
79. Toxicology (3 h.)
80. Going over previous Lectures on Physiology and Osteology (1 h.)
81. Theory and Practice of Midwifery (4 h.)
82. Operations in Midwifery (1 h.)
83. Clinical Study of Cutaneous and Venereal Diseases (3 h.)
84. Use of the Laryngoscope (1 h.)
85. Diseases of the Heart (1 h.)
86. Percussion, Auscultation, etc. (3 h.)
87. Auscultation, Percussion, and use of the Laryngoscope (4 h.)
88. General and Special Surgery.
89. Physiology of Animal Generation (1 h.)
90. Physiology of the Nerves and Muscles (4 h.)
91. Hernia (1 h.)
92. Puncture with Experiments (1 h.)
93. Hereditary Vices (1 h.)
94. General and Special Surgery (4 h.)
95. Auscultation, Percussion, etc. (1 h.)
96. Diagnostics (2 h.)
97. Use of Electricity in Medicine (1 h.)
98. Experimental Physiology (2 h.)

99. Going over previous Lectures on different points of Physiology (1 h.)
100. Ophthalmology (3 h.)
101. Use of the Ophthalmoscope (1 h.)
102. Diagnostics of abnormal states of the Eye (1 h.)
103. Theory and Practice of Midwifery (4 h.)
104. Operations in Midwifery (1 h.)
105. Thermal Waters (2 h.)
106. Going over previous Lectures on Pharmacology (1 h.)
107. Position of the *Viscera* in the Human Body (1 h.)
108. The Laryngoscope (1 h.)
109. The Laryngoscope, Auscultation, Inhalations, etc. (1 h.)
110. Cure of Insanity; the Diseases of the Brain (2 h.)

IV. Faculty of Philosophy.

Full Professors.

1. Æschines *in Ctesiphontem* (2 h.)
2. Palæontology (5 h.)
3. Greek Antiquities (6 h.)
4. Botany (1 h.)
5. Special Botany (4 h.)
6. *Cryptogama, etc.* (1 h.)
7. Meteorology (1 h.)
8. Experimental Physics (4 h.)
9. Grecian History (4 h.)
10. Modern History, from 1718 to 1815 (5 h.)
11. Archæology (2 h.)

APPENDIX. 239

12. Greek Mythology (1 h.)
13. National Economy (4 h.)
14. Science of Finance (4 h.)
15. The *Persæ* of Æschylus (4 h.)
16. The *Miles Gloriosus* of Plautus (4 h.)
17. Politics and Political Economy (1 h.)
18. Principles of Political Economy (4 h.)
19. Logic and Metaphysics (4 h.)
20. Political Economy; Theory of Finance (4 h.)
21. Organic Chemistry (1 h.)
22. Experimental Chemistry (3 h.)
23. The Speeches of Lysias (2 h.)
24. The Homeric Poems, and particularly the *Odyssey* (4 h.)
25. Surfaces of the Fourth Order (1 h.)
26. Analytical Mechanics (4 h.)
27. History of Egypt (1 h.)
28. Grammar of Hieroglyphics (3 h.)
29. Explanation of Egyptian Monuments (1 h.)
30. Physical Experiments (1 h.)
31. The 41st book of Livy, and onwards (1 h.)
32. Latin Inscriptions (4 h.)
33. Monuments of the Ancient German Language explained (1 h.)
34. History of the Ancient Poetry of Germany (4 h.)
35. The *Germany* of Tacitus (4 h.)
36. Analysis of Determinate Numbers (3 h.)
37. General and Special Geology (6 h.)
38. Zootomy (4 h.)
39. Historical Exercises (1 h.)

40. Modern History of England and of her Parliament (4 h.)
41. History of Politics (1 h.)
42. The Syriac Language (1 h.)
43. Grammar of the Semitic Languages (1 h.)
44. Explanation of the Psalms (5 h.)
45. Principles of Arabic Grammar (3 h.)
46. Comparison of Persian with Sanscrit (1 h.)
47. Crystallography (1 h.)
48. Mineralogy (6 h.)
49. The sixth book of Aristotle's *Nicomach. Eth.* (2 h.)
50. Psychology (4 h.)
51. History of Philosophy (5 h.)
52. Theory of Analytical Functions (6 h.)
53. Algebraical Equations (6 h.)

Assistant Professors.

54. History of Modern Philosophy (2 h.)
55. Logic (4 h.)
56. General History of Philosophy in 17th century (4 h.)
57. Theory of Determinants (2 h.)
58. Algebra (4 h.)
59. Differential Calculus (4 h.)
60. Physical Geography, and History of the Mediterranean (3 h.)
61. Simple Drugs examined with the Microscope (1 h.)
62. Botany of Medical Plants (6 h.)

63. Pharmacognosy (4 h.)
64. Certain Arabic Authors explained (1 h.)
65. Arabic Grammar (3 h.)
66. The book of Genesis (5 h.)
67. Theory of Geographical Phenomena (3 h.)
68. Analytical Mechanics (1 h.)
69. History of Astronomy (2 h.)
70. Theory of the motion of Planets and Comets (4 h.)
71. Exercises in Archæology (1 h.)
72. History of Greek Sculpture (3 h.)
73. National Economy (4 h.)
74. The *Epidicus* of Plautus (2 h.)
75. Roman Antiquities (4 h.)
76. History of Greek Philosophy (2 h.)
77. Æsthetics (2 h.)
78. Select Epistles of Cicero (1 h.)
79. Philological Exercises (1 h.)
80. Greek Mythology (3 h.)
81. Exercises in Palæography (1 h.)
82. Latin Palæography (1 h.)
83. National History of Glumaceous Plants (1 h.)
84. Systems of Medical Plants (6 h.)
85. Exercises in Anatomy and Physiology (4 h.)
86. Ancient Geography (3 h.)
87. Botany, Diseases of Plants (4 h.)
88. Agronomical Science (1 h.)
89. Historical Exercises (1 h.)
90. History of Germany (4 h.)
91. Art of Singing, especially Church Singing (2 h.)

92. Musical Composition (4 h.)
93. Pædagogy (2 h.)
94. The *Nibelungen* (6 h.)
95. Exercises in deciphering Manuscripts (1 h.)
96. Logic; Encyclopædia of Philosophical Sciences (4 h.)
97. History of Philosophy (4 h.)
98. History of the New World (2 h.)
99. Geography and Ethnography of Europe (4 h.)
100. The Chaldee Language (1 h.)
101. History of the Armenians (3 h.)
102. General History of Physics since Galileo (2 h.)
103. Theory of Electricity (1 h.)
104. Physics applied to Mathematics, Acoustics (4 h.)
105. Chemical Metallurgy (3 h.)
106. Principles of Qualitative and Quantitative Analysis (1 h.)
107. Experimental Chemistry (6 h.)
108. Pharmacy (3 h.)
109. Chemical Experiments (8 h. *daily*)
110. The Turkish Language (3 h.)
111. Principles of National Psychology (1 h.)
112. Philosophy of Language; General Grammar (4 h.)
113. Character of the Indo-Germanic Languages (4 h.)
114. Universal History of the Arts (5 h.)
115. The *Sacontala* of Calidâsa (2 h.)
116. Sanscrit Grammar (3 h.)
117. Zend or Pâli Grammar (2 h.)

APPENDIX. 243

118. The Rigveda or the Atharvaveda explained (1 h.)
119. Course of Sanscrit, Zend, or Pâli (1 h.)
120. The Dramatic Art (1 h.)
121. Psychology and Anthropology (3 h.)

Privatdocenten.

122. Experimental Organic Chemistry (4 h.)
123. Experiments in Organic Chemistry (6 h.)
124. Schleiermacher (1 h.)
125. Logic, and Encyclopædia of the Philosophical Sciences (4 h.)
126. The Limits between Poetry and Philosophy (1 h.)
127. The American Political Economist, Henry Carey.
128. Logic and Metaphysics.
129. Political Economy.
130. History of Modern Civilisation.
131. Agronomical Zoology (3 h.)[1]
132. Entomology (3 h.)
133. The Koran (2 h.)
134. The Semitic Dialects (1 h.)
135. Differential Calculus (4 h.)
136. Analytical Geometry (4 h.)
137. The Bhagvatgita (1 h.)
138. Panini's Sanscrit Grammar (3 h.)
139. Hindustani or Pâli Grammar (2 h.)
140. Indian Philosophy (1 h.)
141. The Satires of Juvenal (2 h.)

[1] This course treats of the animals which do harm to agriculture.

142. Syntax of the Latin Language (4 h.)
143. Lucretius, *De Rerum Natura* (1 h.)
144. Rhetoric and Rhetorical Exercises (2 h.)
145. Aristotle, and the Natural Philosophy of the Ancients (4 h.)
146. History of the German Universities (1 h.)
147. Systems of Modern Philosophy since Kant (4 h.)
148. Experimental Chemistry (6 h.)
149. The Olynthiac Orations of Demosthenes (1 h.)
150. The Epistles of Horace (4 h.)
151. Physics applied to Mathematics, Acoustics, Optics, etc. (3 h.)
152. General Geology.
153. Natural History of *Entozoa* (1 h.)
154. General Zoology.
155. The Climate of Italy (1 h.)
156. Medical Climatology (2 h.)
157. Conversational Lecture on Chemistry (1 h.)
158. History of Chemistry (1 h.)
159. Qualitative and Quantitative part of Analytical Chemistry (3 h.)
160. Medico-Legal Chemistry (3 h.)
161. Chemical Experiments (8 h. *daily*).
162. Theory of Irrigation and Drainage (1 h.)
163. Principals of Agriculture (3 h.)
164. Management of Cattle (3 h.)
165. Book-keeping (1 h.)

Readers (for Modern Languages).
166. Lectures in Italian on Italian Literature (2 h.)

167. Italian Grammar (2 h.)
168. Lectures on the Italian and French Languages (2 h.)
169. German Shorthand (2 h.)
170. German, English, French, and Italian Shorthand (2 h.)
171. Lectures in Polish on Persian Grammar and the Zend Language (2 h.)
172. The Turkish Language ; *Kirk Vezir* read (3 h.)
173. Practical Lectures on the Persian and Turkish Languages (2 h.)
174. Lectures in English on English Literature down to the 16th century (1 h.)
175. Lectures in the English Language (2 h.)

THE END.

Printed by R. & R. CLARK, *Edinburgh.*

BY THE SAME AUTHOR.

The Complete Poetical Works.
New Edition, with additional Poems. Two Vols. Crown 8vo. 7s. 6d. each. Vol. I.—Early Poems, Narrative Poems, and Sonnets. Vol. II.—Lyric, Dramatic, and Elegiac Poems.

A French Eton; or, Middle-Class Education and the State. Fcap. 8vo. 2s. 6d.

Essays in Criticism. Third Edition, revised and enlarged. Crown 8vo. 9s.

Isaiah XL.—LXVI. With the Shorter Prophecies allied to it. Arranged and Edited with Notes. Crown 8vo. 5s.

A Bible-Reading for Schools.
The Great Prophecy of Israel's Restoration (Isaiah, Chapters 40-66.) Arranged and Edited for Young Learners. Fourth Edition. 18mo. 1s.

Selected Poems. Golden Treasury Series.
4s. 6d. Large Paper Edition. Crown 8vo. 12s. 6d.

Poetry of Byron.
Chosen and arranged by MATTHEW ARNOLD. Large Paper Edition. 9s.

Poems of Wordsworth.
Chosen and Edited by MATTHEW ARNOLD. With Portrait. Large Paper Edition. 9s.

Letters, Tracts, and Speeches on Irish Affairs. By EDMUND BURKE. Arranged and Edited by MATTHEW ARNOLD, with a Preface. Crown 8vo. 6s.

Johnson's Lives of the Poets.
The Six Chief Lives, with Macaulay's "Life of Johnson." Edited, with a Preface, by MATTHEW ARNOLD. Crown 8vo. 6s.

MACMILLAN AND CO., LONDON, W.C.

MESSRS. MACMILLAN & CO.'S PUBLICATIONS.

By JOHN RICHARD GREEN, M.A., LL.D.

A Short History of the English People.
With Coloured Maps, Genealogical Tables, and Chronological Annals. Crown 8vo. 8s. 6d. 80th Thousand.

Stray Studies from England and Italy.
Crown 8vo. 8s. 6d.

The Making of England.
With Maps. 8vo. 16s.

History of the English People.
In Four Vols. 8vo.
Vol. I.—EARLY ENGLAND, 449-1071—Foreign Kings, 1071-1214—The Charter, 1204-1291—The Parliament, 1307-1461. With Eight Coloured Maps. 8vo. 16s.
Vol. II.—The Monarchy, 1461-1540—The Reformation, 1540-160?. 8vo. 16s.
Vol. III.—Puritan England, 1603-1660—The Revolution, 1660-1688. With Four Maps. 8vo. 16s.
Vol. IV.—The Revolution, 1683-1760—Modern England, 1760-1815. With Maps and Index.

Readings from English History.
Selected and Edited by. In Three Parts. Fcap. 8vo. 1s. 6d. each. Part I.—From Hengest to Cressy. Part II.—From Cressy to Cromwell. Part III.—From Cromwell to Balaklava.

Essays of Joseph Addison.
Chosen and Edited by. 18mo. 4s. 6d. (*Golden Treasury Series.*)

A Short Geography of the British Islands.
By JOHN RICHARD GREEN and ALICE STOPFORD GREEN. With twenty-eight Maps. Fcap. 8vo. 3s. 6d.

The Teacher.
Hints on School Management. A Handbook for Managers, Teachers' Assistants, and Pupil Teachers. By J. R. BLAKISTON, M.A. Crown 8vo. 2s. 6d.

On Teaching; its Ends and Means.
A Book for Teachers and Parents. By Prof. CALDERWOOD. Third Edition. With Additional Chapter on "Home Training." 2s. 6d.

School Inspection.
By D. R. FEARON, M.A., Assistant Commissioner of Endowed Schools. Third Edition. Crown 8vo. 2s. 6d.

MACMILLAN AND CO., LONDON, W.C.

BEDFORD STREET, COVENT GARDEN, LONDON,
September, 1881.

MACMILLAN & CO.'S CATALOGUE of WORKS in MATHEMATICS and PHYSICAL SCIENCE; including PURE and APPLIED MATHEMATICS; PHYSICS, ASTRONOMY, GEOLOGY, CHEMISTRY, ZOOLOGY, BOTANY; and of WORKS in MENTAL and MORAL PHILOSOPHY and Allied Subjects.

MATHEMATICS.

Airy.—Works by Sir G. B. AIRY, K.C.B., Astronomer Royal:—
ELEMENTARY TREATISE ON PARTIAL DIFFERENTIAL EQUATIONS. Designed for the Use of Students in the Universities. With Diagrams. New Edition. Crown 8vo. 5s. 6d.
ON THE ALGEBRAICAL AND NUMERICAL THEORY OF ERRORS OF OBSERVATIONS AND THE COMBINATION OF OBSERVATIONS. Second Edition. Crown 8vo. 6s. 6d.
UNDULATORY THEORY OF OPTICS. Designed for the Use of Students in the University. New Edition. Crown 8vo. 6s. 6d.
ON SOUND AND ATMOSPHERIC VIBRATIONS. With the Mathematical Elements of Music. Designed for the Use of Students of the University. Second Edition, revised and enlarged. Crown 8vo. 9s.
A TREATISE ON MAGNETISM. Designed for the Use of Students in the University. Crown 8vo. 9s. 6d.

Alexander.—ELEMENTARY APPLIED MECHANICS. By THOMAS ALEXANDER, C.E., Professor of Civil Engineering in the Imperial College of Engineering, Tokei, Japan. Crown 8vo. 4s. 6d.

Ball (R. S., A.M.).—EXPERIMENTAL MECHANICS. A Course of Lectures delivered at the Royal College of Science for Ireland. By ROBERT STAWELL BALL, A.M., Professor of Applied Mathematics and Mechanics in the Royal College of Science for Ireland (Science and Art Department). Cheaper Issue. Royal 8vo. 10s. 6d.

Bayma.—THE ELEMENTS OF MOLECULAR MECHANICS. By JOSEPH BAYMA, S.J., Professor of Philosophy, Stonyhurst College. Demy 8vo. 10s. 6d.

Boole.—Works by G. BOOLE, D.C.L, F.R.S., Professor of Mathematics in the Queen's University, Ireland :—
A TREATISE ON DIFFERENTIAL EQUATIONS. Third Edition. Edited by I. TODHUNTER. Crown 8vo. 14s.
A TREATISE ON DIFFERENTIAL EQUATIONS. Supplementary Volume. Edited by I. TODHUNTER. Crown 8vo. 8s. 6d.
THE CALCULUS OF FINITE DIFFERENCES. Third Edition. Edited by J. F. MOULTON, late Fellow of Christ's College, Cambridge. Crown 8vo. 10s. 6d.

Chalmers.—GRAPHICAL DETERMINATION OF FORCES IN ENGINEERING STRUCTURES. By JAMES B. CHALMERS, C.E. With Illustrations. 8vo. 24s.

Cheyne.—AN ELEMENTARY TREATISE ON THE PLANETARY THEORY. With a Collection of Problems. By C. H. H. CHEYNE, M.A., F.R.A.S. Second Edition. Crown 8vo. 6s. 6d.

Clausius.—THE MECHANICAL THEORY OF HEAT. By R. CLAUSIUS. Translated by WALTER R. BROWNE, M.A., late Fellow of Trinity College, Cambridge. Crown 8vo. 10s. 6d.

Clifford.—THE ELEMENTS OF DYNAMIC. An Introduction to the study of Motion and Rest in Solid and Fluid Bodies. By W. K. CLIFFORD, F.R.S., Professor of Applied Mathematics and Mechanics at University College, London. Part I.—Kinematic. Crown 8vo. 7s. 6d.

Cumming.—AN INTRODUCTION TO THE THEORY OF ELECTRICITY. With numerous Examples. By LINNÆUS CUMMING, M.A., Assistant Master at Rugby School. Crown 8vo. 8s. 6d.

Cuthbertson.—EUCLIDIAN GEOMETRY. By F. CUTHBERTSON, M.A., Head Mathematical Master of the City of London School. Extra fcap. 8vo. 4s. 6d.

MATHEMATICS. 3

Everett.—UNITS AND PHYSICAL CONSTANTS. By J. D. EVERETT, M.A., D.C.L., F.R.S., Professor of Natural Philosophy, Queen's College, Belfast. Extra fcap. 8vo. 4s. 6d.

Ferrers.—Works by the Rev. N. M. FERRERS, M.A., F.R.S., Master and Fellow of Gonville and Caius College, Cambridge:—

AN ELEMENTARY TREATISE ON TRILINEAR CO-ORDI-NATES, the Method of Reciprocal Polars, and the Theory of Projectors. Third Edition, revised. Crown 8vo. 6s. 6d.

SPHERICAL HARMONICS AND SUBJECTS CONNECTED WITH THEM. Crown 8vo. 7s. 6d.

Frost.—Works by PERCIVAL FROST, M.A., late Fellow of St. John's College, Mathematical Lecturer of King's Coll. Cambridge:—

THE FIRST THREE SECTIONS OF NEWTON'S PRIN-CIPIA. With Notes and Illustrations. Also a Collection of Problems, principally intended as Examples of Newton's Methods. Third Edition. 8vo. 12s.

AN ELEMENTARY TREATISE ON CURVE TRACING. 8vo. 12s.

SOLID GEOMETRY. Being a New Edition, revised and enlarged, of the Treatise by FROST and WOLSTENHOLME. Vol. I. 8vo. 16s.

Godfray.—Works by HUGH GODFRAY, M.A., Mathematical Lecturer at Pembroke College, Cambridge:—

A TREATISE ON ASTRONOMY, for the Use of Colleges and Schools. 8vo. 12s. 6d.

AN ELEMENTARY TREATISE ON THE LUNAR THEORY, with a Brief Sketch of the Problem up to the time of Newton. Second Edition, revised. Crown 8vo. 5s. 6d.

Green (George).—MATHEMATICAL PAPERS OF THE LATE GEORGE GREEN, Fellow of Gonville and Caius College, Cambridge. Edited by N. M. FERRERS, M.A., Fellow and Master of Gonville and Caius College. 8vo. 15s.

Hemming.—AN ELEMENTARY TREATISE ON THE DIFFERENTIAL AND INTEGRAL CALCULUS. For the Use of Colleges and Schools. By G. W. HEMMING, M.A., Fellow of St. John's College, Cambridge. Second Edition, with Corrections and Additions. 8vo. 9s.

Jackson.—GEOMETRICAL CONIC SECTIONS. An Elementary Treatise in which the Conic Sections are defined as the Plane Sections of a Cone, and treated by the Method of Projections. By J. STUART JACKSON, M.A., late Fellow of Gonville and Caius College. Crown 8vo. 4s. 6d.

Kelland and Tait.—AN INTRODUCTION TO QUATERNIONS. With numerous Examples. By P. KELLAND, M.A., F.R.S., and P. G. TAIT, M.A., Professors in the department of Mathematics in the University of Edinburgh. Crown 8vo. 7s. 6d.

Kempe.—HOW TO DRAW A STRAIGHT LINE. A Lecture on Linkages. By A.B. KEMPE, B.A. Illustrated. Crown 8vo. 1s.6d.
[*Nature Series.*

Merriman.—ELEMENTS OF THE METHOD OF LEAST SQUARES. By MANSFIELD MERRIMAN, Professor of Civil and Mechanical Engineering, Lehigh University, Bethlehem, Penn., U.S.A. Crown 8vo. 7s. 6d.

Morgan.—A COLLECTION OF PROBLEMS AND EXAMPLES IN MATHEMATICS. With Answers. By H. A. MORGAN, M.A., Sadlerian and Mathematical Lecturer of Jesus College, Cambridge. Crown 8vo. 6s. 6d.

Newton's Principia.—4to. 31s. 6d.
It is a sufficient guarantee of the reliability of this complete edition of Newton's Principia *that it has been printed for and under the care of Professor Sir William Thomson and Professor Blackburn, of Glasgow University.*

Parkinson.—Works by S. PARKINSON, D.D., F.R.S., Fellow and Tutor of St. John's College, Cambridge.
A TREATISE ON OPTICS. Third Edition, revised and enlarged. Crown 8vo. cloth. 10s. 6d.
A TREATISE ON ELEMENTARY MECHANICS. For the Use of the Junior Classes at the University and the Higher Classes in Schools. With a Collection of Examples. Sixth Edition, revised. Crown 8vo. 9s. 6d.

Phear.—ELEMENTARY HYDROSTATICS. With Numerous Examples. By J. B. PHEAR, M.A., Fellow and late Assistant Tutor of Clare Coll. Cambridge. Fourth Edition. Cr. 8vo. cloth. 5s. 6d.

Pirie.—LESSONS ON RIGID DYNAMICS. By the Rev. G. PIRIE, M.A., Fellow and Tutor of Queen's College, Cambridge. Crown 8vo. 6s.

Puckle.—AN ELEMENTARY TREATISE ON CONIC SECTIONS AND ALGEBRAIC GEOMETRY. With numerous Examples and Hints for their Solution. By G. HALE PUCKLE, M.A. Fourth Edition, enlarged. Crown 8vo. 7s. 6d.

MATHEMATICS.

Rayleigh.—THE THEORY OF SOUND. By LORD RAYLEIGH, F.R.S., formerly Fellow of Trinity College, Cambridge. 8vo. Vol. I. 12s. 6d.; Vol. II. 12s. 6d.   [Vol. III. *in preparation.*

Reuleaux.—THE KINEMATICS OF MACHINERY. Outlines of a Theory of Machines. By Professor F. REULEAUX. Translated and edited by A. B. W. KENNEDY, C.E., Professor of Civil and Mechanical Engineering, University College, London. With 450 Illustrations. Royal 8vo. 20s.

Routh.—Works by EDWARD JOHN ROUTH, M.A., F.R.S., late Fellow and Assistant Tutor of St. Peter's College, Cambridge; Examiner in the University of London :—

AN ELEMENTARY TREATISE ON THE DYNAMICS OF THE SYSTEM OF RIGID BODIES. With numerous Examples. Third Edition, enlarged. 8vo. 21s.

STABILITY OF A GIVEN STATE OF MOTION, PARTICULARLY STEADY MOTION. The Adams' Prize Essay for 1877. 8vo. 8s. 6d.

Tait and Steele.—DYNAMICS OF A PARTICLE. With numerous Examples. By Professor TAIT and Mr. STEELE. Fourth Edition, revised. Crown 8vo. 12s.

Thomson.—PAPERS ON ELECTROSTATICS AND MAGNETISM. By Professor SIR WILLIAM THOMSON, F.R.S. 8vo. 18s.

Todhunter.—Works by I. TODHUNTER, M.A., F.R.S., of St. John's College, Cambridge :—

"*Mr. Todhunter is chiefly known to students of mathematics as the author of a series of admirable mathematical text-books, which possess the rare qualities of being clear in style and absolutely free from mistakes, typographical or other.*"—Saturday Review.

A TREATISE ON SPHERICAL TRIGONOMETRY. New Edition, enlarged. Crown 8vo. 4s. 6d.

PLANE CO-ORDINATE GEOMETRY, as applied to the Straight Line and the Conic Sections. With numerous Examples. New Edition. Crown 8vo. 7s. 6d.

A TREATISE ON THE DIFFERENTIAL CALCULUS. With numerous Examples. New Edition. Crown 8vo. 10s. 6d.

A TREATISE ON THE INTEGRAL CALCULUS AND ITS APPLICATIONS. With numerous Examples. New Edition, revised and enlarged. Crown 8vo. 10s. 6d.

Todhunter—*continued.*

EXAMPLES OF ANALYTICAL GEOMETRY OF THREE DIMENSIONS. New Edition, revised. Crown 8vo. cloth. 4s.

A TREATISE ON ANALYTICAL STATICS. With numerous Examples. New Edition, revised and enlarged. Crown 8vo. cloth. 10s. 6d.

A HISTORY OF THE MATHEMATICAL THEORY OF PROBABILITY, from the Time of Pascal to that of Laplace. 8vo. 18s.

RESEARCHES IN THE CALCULUS OF VARIATIONS, Principally on the Theory of Discontinuous Solutions: An Essay to which the Adams' Prize was awarded in the University of Cambridge in 1871. 8vo. 6s.

A HISTORY OF THE MATHEMATICAL THEORIES OF ATTRACTION, and the Figure of the Earth, from the time of Newton to that of Laplace. Two vols. 8vo. 24s.

AN ELEMENTARY TREATISE ON LAPLACE'S, LAME'S, AND BESSEL'S FUNCTIONS. Crown 8vo. 10s. 6d.

Wilson (W. P.).—A TREATISE ON DYNAMICS. By W. P. WILSON, M.A., Fellow of St. John's College, Cambridge, and Professor of Mathematics in Queen's College, Belfast. 8vo. 9s. 6d.

Wolstenholme.—MATHEMATICAL PROBLEMS, on Subjects included in the First and Second Divisions of the Schedule of Subjects for the Cambridge Mathematical Tripos Examination. Devised and arranged by JOSEPH WOLSTENHOLME, late Fellow of Christ's College, sometime Fellow of St. John's College, and Professor of Mathematics in the Royal Indian Engineering College. New Edition, greatly enlarged. 8vo. 18s.

Young.—SIMPLE PRACTICAL METHODS OF CALCULATING STRAINS ON GIRDERS, ARCHES, AND TRUSSES. With a Supplementary Essay on Economy in suspension Bridges. By E. W. YOUNG, Associate of King's College, London, and Member of the Institution of Civil Engineers. 8vo. 7s. 6d.

PHYSICAL SCIENCE.

Airy (G. B.).—POPULAR ASTRONOMY. With Illustrations. By Sir G. B. AIRY, K.C.B., Astronomer Royal. New Edition. fcap. 8vo. 4s. 6d.

Balfour.—A TREATISE ON COMPARATIVE EMBRYOLOGY. By F. M. BALFOUR, M.A., F.R.S., Fellow and Lecturer of Trinity College, Cambridge. With Illustrations. In Two Volumes. 8vo. Vol. I. 18s. Vol. II. 21s.

Bastian.—Works by H. CHARLTON BASTIAN, M.D., F.R.S., Professor of Pathological Anatomy in University College, London, &c.:—

THE BEGINNINGS OF LIFE: Being some Account of the Nature, Modes of Origin, and Transformations of Lower Organisms. In Two Volumes. With upwards of 100 Illustrations. Crown 8vo. 28s.

EVOLUTION AND THE ORIGIN OF LIFE. Crown 8vo. 6s. 6d.

Bettany.—FIRST LESSONS IN PRACTICAL BOTANY. By G. T. BETTANY, M.A., B.Sc., F.R.S., Lecturer on Botany in Guy's Hospital Medical School. 18mo. 1s.

Blake.—ASTRONOMICAL MYTHS. Based on Flammarion's "The Heavens." By John F. BLAKE. With numerous Illustrations. Crown 8vo. 9s.

Blanford (H. F.).—RUDIMENTS OF PHYSICAL GEOGRAPHY FOR THE USE OF INDIAN SCHOOLS. By H. F. BLANFORD, F.G.S. With numerous Illustrations and Glossary of Technical Terms employed. New Edition. Globe 8vo. 2s. 6d.

Blanford (W. T.).—GEOLOGY AND ZOOLOGY OF ABYSSINIA. By W. T. BLANFORD. 8vo. 21s.

Brodie.—IDEAL CHEMISTRY. A LECTURE. By Sir B. C. BRODIE, Bart., D.C.L., F.R.S., Professor of Chemistry in the University of Oxford. Crown 8vo. 2s.

Brunton.—Works by T. LAUDER BRUNTON, M.D., F.R.C P., F.R.S., Assistant Physician and Lecturer on Materia Medica and Therapeutics at St. Bartholomew's Hospital.

PHARMACOLOGY AND THERAPEUTICS; or Medicine Past and Present. The Goulstonian Lectures delivered before the Royal College of Physicians in 1871. Crown 8vo. 6s.

THE BIBLE AND SCIENCE. With Illustrations. Crown 8vo. 10s. 6d.

Bosanquet.—AN ELEMENTARY TREATISE ON MUSICAL INTERVALS AND TEMPERAMENT. With an Account of an Enharmonic Harmonium exhibited in the Loan Collection of Scientific Instruments, South Kensington, 1876; also of an Enharmonic Organ exhibited to the Musical Association of London, May, 1875. By R. H. Bosanquet, Fellow of St. John's College, Oxford. 8vo. 6s.

Challenger.—Report on the Scientific Results on the Voyage of H.M.S. "Challenger," during the Years 1873-76. Under the command of Captain Sir GEORGE NARES, R.N., F.R.S., and Captain FRANK TURLE THOMSON, R.N. Prepared under the Superintendence of Sir C. WYVILLE THOMSON, Knt., F.R.S., &c. Regius Professor of Natural History in the University of Edinburgh; Director of the Civilian Scientific Staff on board. With Illustrations. Published by order of Her Majesty's Government.

Volume I. Zoology. Royal. 37s. 6d. Or,
Part. I. Report on the Brachiopoda, 2s. 6d.
 II. Report on the Pennatulida, 4s.
 III. Report on the Ostracoda, 15s.
 IV. Report on the Bones of Cetacea, 2s.
 V. The Development of the Green Turtle, 4s. 6d.
 VI. Report on the Shore Fishes, 10s.
Volume II. Zoology. Royal. 50s. Or,
Part VII. Report on the Corals. 15s.
 VIII. Report on the Birds. 35s.

Cleland.—EVOLUTION, EXPRESSION AND SENSATION, CELL LIFE AND PATHOLOGY. By JOHN CLELAND, M.D., F.R.S., Professor of Anatomy in the University of Glasgow. Crown 8vo. 5s.

Clifford.—SEEING AND THINKING. By the late Professor W. K. CLIFFORD, F.R.S. With Diagrams. Crown 8vo. 3s. 6d.
[*Nature Series.*

Coal: ITS HISTORY AND ITS USES. By Professors GREEN, MIALL, THORPE, RÜCKER, and MARSHALL, of the Yorkshire College, Leeds. With Illustrations. 8vo. 12s. 6d.

Cooke (Josiah P., Jun.).—FIRST PRINCIPLES OF CHEMICAL PHILOSOPHY. By JOSIAH P. COOKE, Jun., Ervine Professor of Chemistry and Mineralogy in Harvard College. Third Edition, revised and corrected. Crown 8vo. 12s.

Cooke (M. C.).—HANDBOOK OF BRITISH FUNGI, with full descriptions of all the Species, and Illustrations of the Genera. By M. C. COOKE, M.A. Two vols. crown 8vo. 24s.

PHYSICAL SCIENCE. 9

Crossley.—HANDBOOK OF DOUBLE STARS, WITH A CATALOGUE OF 1,200 DOUBLE STARS AND EXTENSIVE LISTS OF MEASURES FOR THE USE OF AMATEURS. By E. CROSSLEY, F.R.A.S., J. GLEDHILL, F.R.A.S., and J. M. WILSON, F.R.A.S. With Illustrations. 8vo. 21s.
CORRECTIONS TO THE HANDBOOK OF DOUBLE STARS. 8vo. 1s.

Dawkins.—Works by W. BOYD DAWKINS, F.R.S., &c., Professor of Geology and Palæontology at Owens College, Manchester.
CAVE-HUNTING : Researches on the Evidence of Caves respecting the Early Inhabitants of Europe. With Coloured Plate and Woodcuts. 8vo. 21s.
EARLY MAN IN BRITAIN, AND HIS PLACE IN THE TERTIARY PERIOD. With Illustrations. 8vo. 25s.

Dawson (J. W.).—ACADIAN GEOLOGY. The Geologic Structure, Organic Remains, and Mineral Resources of Nova Scotia, New Brunswick, and Prince Edward Island. By JOHN WILLIAM DAWSON, M.A., LL.D., F.R.S., F.G.S., Principal and Vice-Chancellor of M'Gill College and University, Montreal, &c. With a Geological Map and numerous Illustrations. Third Edition, with Supplement. 8vo. 21s. Supplement, separately, 2s. 6d.

Fiske.—DARWINISM; AND OTHER ESSAYS. By JOHN FISKE, M.A., LL.D., formerly Lecturer on Philosophy in Harvard University. Crown 8vo. 7s. 6d.

Fleischer.—A SYSTEM OF VOLUMETRIC ANALYSIS. By Dr. E. FLEISCHER. Translated from the Second German Edition by M. M. Pattison Muir, F.R.S.E., with Notes and Additions. Illustrated. Crown 8vo. 7s. 6d.

Flower.—FASHION IN DEFORMITY, as Illustrated in the Customs of Barbarous and Civilized Races. By WILLIAM HENRY FLOWER, LL.D., M.D., F.R.S., &c., Hunterian Professor of Comparative Anatomy, and Conservator of the Museum of the Royal College of Surgeons of England. With numerous Illustrations. Crown 8vo. 2s. 6d. [Nature Series.

Flückiger and Hanbury.—PHARMACOGRAPHIA. A History of the Principal Drugs of Vegetable Origin met with in Great Britain and India. By F. A. FLÜCKIGER, M.D., and D. HANBURY, F.R.S. Second Edition, revised. 8vo. 21s.

Forbes.—THE TRANSIT OF VENUS. By GEORGE FORBES, B.A., Professor of Natural Philosophy in the Andersonian University of Glasgow. With numerous Illustrations. Crown 8vo. 3s. 6d.
[Nature Series.

Foster.—A TEXT-BOOK OF PHYSIOLOGY. By MICHAEL FOSTER, M.D., F.R.S., Prælector in Physiology, and Fellow of Trinity College, Cambridge. With Illustrations. Third Edition, revised. 8vo. 21s.

Foster and Balfour.—ELEMENTS OF EMBRYOLOGY. By MICHAEL FOSTER, M.D., F.R.S., and F. M. BALFOUR, M.A., Fellow of Trinity College, Cambridge. With numerous Illustrations. Part I. Crown 8vo. 7s. 6d.

Galloway.—THE STEAM ENGINE AND ITS INVENTORS. A Historical Sketch. By ROBERT L. GALLOWAY, Mining Engineer. With numerous Illustrations. Crown 8vo. 10s. 6d.

Galton.—Works by FRANCIS GALTON, F.R.S. :—
METEOROGRAPHICA, or Methods of Mapping the Weather. Illustrated by upwards of 600 Printed Lithographic Diagrams. 4to. 9s.

HEREDITARY GENIUS: An Inquiry into its Laws and Consequences. Demy 8vo. 12s.
The Times *calls it "a most able and most interesting book."*

ENGLISH MEN OF SCIENCE; THEIR NATURE AND NURTURE. 8vo. 8s. 6d.
*" The book is certainly one of very great interest."—*Nature.

Gamgee.—A TEXT-BOOK OF THE PHYSIOLOGICAL CHEMISTRY OF THE ANIMAL BODY. By ARTHUR GAMGEE, M.D., F.R.S., Professor of Physiology in Owens College, Manchester. With Illustrations. In Two Vols. Medium 8vo. Vol. I. 18s. [*Vol. II. in the Press.*

Geikie.—Works by ARCHIBALD GEIKIE, LL.D., F.R.S., Murchison Professor of Geology and Mineralogy at Edinburgh :—

ELEMENTARY LESSONS IN PHYSICAL GEOGRAPHY. With numerous Illustrations. Fcap. 8vo. 4s. 6d. Questions, 1s. 6d.

OUTLINES OF FIELD GEOLOGY. With Illustrations. Crown 8vo. 3s. 6d.

PRIMER OF GEOLOGY. Illustrated. 18mo. 1s.

PRIMER OF PHYSICAL GEOGRAPHY. Illustrated. 18mo. 1s.

TEXT-BOOK OF GEOLOGY. 8vo. [*Immediately.*

PHYSICAL SCIENCE.

Gray.—STRUCTURAL BOTANY, OR ORGANOGRAPHY ON THE BASIS OF MORPHOLOGY. To which are added the principles of Taxonomy and Phytography, and a Glossary of Botanical Terms. By ASA GRAY, LL.D., Fisher Professor of Natural History (Botany) in Harvard University. With numerous Illustrations. 8vo. 10s. 6d.

Green.—A SHORT GEOGRAPHY OF THE BRITISH ISLANDS. By JOHN RICHARD GREEN and ALICE STOPFORD GREEN. With Maps. Fcap. 8vo. 3s. 6d.

The Times says:—" The method of the work, so far as real instruction is concerned, is nearly all that could be desired. . . . Its great merit, in addition to its scientific arrangement and the attractive style so familiar to the readers of Green's 'Short History' is that the facts are so presented as to compel the careful student to think for himself. . . . . The work may be read with pleasure and profit by anyone; we trust that it will gradually find its way into the higher forms of our schools. With this text-book as his guide, an intelligent teacher might make geography what it really is—one of the most interesting and widely-instructive studies."

Grove.—A DICTOINARY OF MUSIC AND MUSICIANS (A.D. 1450—1881). By Eminent Writers, English and Foreign. With Illustrations. Edited by GEORGE GROVE, D.C.L. In 3 vols., 8vo. Parts I. to XIV. 3s. 6d. each. Vols. I. and II. 21s. each. Vol. I. A to IMPROMPTU. Vol. II. IMPROPERIA to PLAIN SONG.

Guillemin.—THE FORCES OF NATURE: A Popular Introduction to the Study of Physical Phenomena. By AMÉDÉE GUILLEMIN. Translated from the French by MRS. NORMAN LOCKYER; and Edited, with Additions and Notes, by J. NORMAN LOCKYER, F.R.S. Illustrated by Coloured Plates, and 455 Woodcuts. Third and cheaper Edition. Royal 8vo. 21s.

" Altogether, the work may be said to have no parallel, either in point of fulness or attraction, as a popular manual of physical science."—Saturday Review.

THE APPLICATIONS OF PHYSICAL FORCES. By A. GUILLEMIN. Translated from the French by Mrs. LOCKYER, and Edited with Notes and Additions by J. N. LOCKYER, F.R.S. With Coloured Plates and numerous Illustrations. New and Cheaper Edition. Imperial 8vo. cloth, extra gilt. 21s.

"*A book which we can heartily recommend, both on account of the width and soundness of its contents, and also because of the excellence of its print, its illustrations, and external appearance.*"—Westminster Review.

Hanbury.—SCIENCE PAPERS : chiefly Pharmacological and Botanical. By DANIEL HANBURY, F.R.S. Edited, with Memoir, by J. INCE, F.L.S., and Portrait engraved by C. H. JEENS. 8vo. 14s.

Henslow.—THE THEORY OF EVOLUTION OF LIVING THINGS, and Application of the Principles of Evolution to Religion considered as Illustrative of the Wisdom and Beneficence of the Almighty. By the Rev. GEORGE HENSLOW, M.A., F.L.S. Crown 8vo. 6s.

Hooker.—Works by Sir J. D. HOOKER, K.C.S.I., C.B., F.R.S., M.D., D.C.L. :—
THE STUDENT'S FLORA OF THE BRITISH ISLANDS. Second Edition, revised and improved. Globe 8vo. 10s. 6d.
"*Certainly the fullest and most accurate manual of the kind that has yet appeared. Dr. Hooker has shown his characteristic industry and ability in the care and skill which he has thrown into the characters of the plants. These are to a great extent original, and are really admirable for their combination of clearness, brevity, and completeness.*"—Pall Mall Gazette.
PRIMER OF BOTANY. With Illustrations. 18mo. 1s. New Edition, revised and corrected.

Hooker and Ball.—JOURNAL OF A TOUR IN MAROCCO AND THE GREAT ATLAS. By Sir J. D. HOOKER, K.C.S.I., C.B., F.R.S., &c., and JOHN BALL, F.R.S. With Appendices, including a Sketch of the Geology of Marocco. By G. MAW, F.L.S., F.G.S. With Map and Illustrations. 8vo. 21s.
"*This is, without doubt, one of the most interesting and valuable books of travel published for many years.*"—Spectator.

Huxley and Martin.—A COURSE OF PRACTICAL INSTRUCTION IN ELEMENTARY BIOLOGY. By T. H. HUXLEY, LL.D., Sec. R.S., assisted by H. N. MARTIN, B.A., M.B., D.Sc.,Fellow of Christ's College, Cambridge. Crown 8vo. 6s.
"*This is the most thoroughly valuable book to teachers and students of biology which has ever appeared in the English tongue.*"—London Quarterly Review.

PHYSICAL SCIENCE. 13

Huxley (Professor).—LAY SERMONS, ADDRESSES, AND REVIEWS. By T. H. HUXLEY, LL.D., F.R.S. New and Cheaper Edition. Crown 8vo. 7s. 6d.

Fourteen Discourses on the following subjects:—(1) *On the Advisableness of Improving Natural Knowledge:*—(2) *Emancipation—Black and White:*—(3) *A Liberal Education, and where to find it:*—(4) *ScientificEducation:*—(5) *On the Educational Value of the Natural History Sciences:*—(6) *On the Study of Zoology:*—(7) *On the Physical Basis of Life:*—(8) *The Scientific Aspects of Positivism:*—(9) *On a Piece of Chalk:*—(10) *Geological Contemporaneity and Persistent Types of Life:*—(11) *Geological Reform:*—(12) *The Origin of Species:*—(13) *Criticisms on the "Origin of Species:"*—(14) *On Descartes' "Discourse touching the Method of using One's Reason rightly and of seeking Scientific Truth."*

ESSAYS SELECTED FROM "LAY SERMONS, ADDRESSES, AND REVIEWS." Second Edition. Crown 8vo. 1s.

CRITIQUES AND ADDRESSES. 8vo. 10s. 6d.

Contents:—1. *Administrative Nihilism.* 2. *The School Boards: what they can do, and what they may do.* 3. *On Medical Education.* 4. *Yeast.* 5. *On the Formation of Coal.* 6. *On Coral and Coral Reefs.* 7. *On the Methods and Results of Ethnology.* 8. *On some Fixed Points in British Ethnology.* 9. *Palæontology and the Doctrine of Evolution.* 10. *Biogenesis and Abiogenesis.* 11. *Mr. Darwin's Critics.* 12. *The Genealogy of Animals.* 13. *Bishop Berkeley on the Metaphysics of Sensation.*

LESSONS IN ELEMENTARY PHYSIOLOGY. With numerous Illustrations. New Edition. Fcap. 8vo. 4s. 6d.

"*Pure gold throughout.*"—Guardian. "*Unquestionably the clearest and most complete elementary treatise on this subject that we possess in any language.*"—Westminster Review.

AMERICAN ADDRESSES: with a Lecture on the Study of Biology. 8vo. 6s. 6d.

PHYSIOGRAPHY: An Introduction to the Study of Nature. With Coloured Plates and numerous Woodcuts. New and Cheaper Edition. Crown 8vo. 6s.

"*It would be hardly possible to place a more useful or suggestive book in the hands of learners and teachers, or one that is better calculated to make physiography a favourite subject in the science schools.*"—Academy.

INTRODUCTORY PRIMER. 18mo. 1s. [*Science Primers.*

Jellet (John H., B.D.).—A TREATISE ON THE THEORY OF FRICTION. By JOHN H. JELLET, B.D., Senior Fellow of Trinity College, Dublin; President of the Royal Irish Academy. 8vo. 8s. 6d.

Jones.—Works by FRANCIS JONES, F.R.S.E., F.C.S., Chemical Master in the Grammar School, Manchester.
THE OWENS COLLEGE JUNIOR COURSE OF PRACTICAL CHEMISTRY. With Preface by Professor ROSCOE. New Edition. 18mo. With Illustrations. 2s. 6d.
QUESTIONS ON CHEMISTRY. A Series of Problems and Exercises in Inorganic and Organic Chemistry. 18mo. 3s.

Kiepert.—MANUAL OF ANCIENT GEOGRAPHY. Authorised translation from the German of HEINRICH KIEPERT, Ph.D., Member of the Royal Academy of Sciences, Berlin, &c. Crown 8vo. 5s.

"*Dr. Kiepert's 'Atlas of Ancient Geography' is highly esteemed in this country. . . . And this volume, which is intended to serve as an explanatory text, will be welcomed accordingly. . . . Any one who will compare it with the text-books that have been commonly in use will see a greater precision and fulness given to the non-classical portion of the subject—a difference that corresponds to the recent development of our knowledge in this direction. He will also perceive that the distinctions and affinities of race are treated, not exhaustively of course, but adequately; that natural features have given to them a prominent place; the continuity of the present with the past, or, in rarer cases, the interruption of the two being noted; that, generally, the geography of the ancient world is made to assume its proper place as the first part, so to speak, of the geography of the world in which we moderns are living. All this will make the volume very useful as a text-book for learners.*"—Pall Mall Gazette.

"*Altogether the English edition of the 'Manual' will form an indispensable companion to Kiepert's 'Atlas,' now used in many of our leading schools.*"—The Times.

Kingsley.—Works By CHARLES KINGSLEY, Canon of Westminster.
GLAUCUS: OR, THE WONDERS OF THE SHORE. New Edition, with numerous Coloured Plates. Crown 8vo. 6s.
SCIENTIFIC LECTURES AND ESSAYS. Crown 8vo. 6s.
SANITARY AND SOCIAL LECTURES AND ESSAYS. Crown 8vo. 6s.
MADAM HOW AND LADY WHY; or, Lessons in Earth-Lore for Children. Illustrated. Crown 8vo. 6s.

Landauer.—BLOWPIPE ANALYSIS. By J. LANDAUER. Authorised English Edition, by JAMES TAYLOR and W. E. KAY, of the Owens College, Manchester. With Illustrations. Extra fcap. 8vo. 4s. 6d.

PHYSICAL SCIENCE. 15

Langdon.—THE APPLICATION OF ELECTRICITY TO RAILWAY WORKING. By W. E. LANGDON, Member of the Society of Telegraph Engineers. With numerous Illustrations. Extra fcap. 8vo. 4s. 6d.
"*There is no officer in the telegraph service who will not profit by the study of this book.*"—Mining Journal.

Lankester.—DEGENERATION. A Chapter in Darwinism. By Professor E. RAY LANKESTER, F.R.S., Fellow of Exeter College, Oxford. With Illustrations. Crown 8vo. 2s. 6d.
[*Nature Series.*

Lockyer (J. N.).—Works by J. NORMAN LOCKYER, F.R.S.—
ELEMENTARY LESSONS IN ASTRONOMY. With numerous Illustrations. New Edition. Fcap. 8vo. 5s. 6d.
"*The book is full, clear, sound, and worthy of attention, not only as a popular exposition, but as a scientific 'Index.'*"—Athenæum.
THE SPECTROSCOPE AND ITS APPLICATIONS. By J. NORMAN LOCKYER, F.R.S. With Coloured Plate and numerous Illustrations. Second Edition. Crown 8vo. 3s. 6d. [*Nature Series.*
CONTRIBUTIONS TO SOLAR PHYSICS. By J. NORMAN LOCKYER, F.R.S. I. A Popular Account of Inquiries into the Physical Constitution of the Sun, with especial reference to Recent Spectroscopic Researches. II. Communications to the Royal Society of London and the French Academy of Sciences, with Notes. Illustrated by 7 Coloured Lithographic Plates and 175 Woodcuts. Royal 8vo. cloth, extra gilt, price 31s. 6d.
PRIMER OF ASTRONOMY. With Illustrations. 18mo. 1s.

Lockyer and Seabroke.—STAR-GAZING: PAST AND PRESENT. An Introduction to Instrumental Astronomy. By J. N. LOCKYER, F.R.S. Expanded from Shorthand Notes of a Course of Royal Institution Lectures with the assistance of G. M. SEABROKE, F.R.A.S. With numerous Illustrations. Royal 8vo. 21s.
"*A book of great interest and utility to the astronomical student.*"
—Athenæum.

Lubbock.—Works by SIR JOHN LUBBOCK, M.P., F.R.S., D.C.L.
THE ORIGIN AND METAMORPHOSES OF INSECTS. With numerous Illustrations. Second Edition. Crown 8vo. 3s. 6d.
[*Nature Series.*
ON BRITISH WILD FLOWERS CONSIDERED IN RELATION TO INSECTS. With Numerous Illustrations. Second Edition. Crown 8vo. 4s. 6d. [*Nature Series.*
SCIENTIFIC LECTURES. With Illustrations. 8vo. 8s. 6d.
CONTENTS:—*Flowers and Insects—Plants and Insects—The Habits of Ants—Introduction to the Study of Prehistoric Archæology*, &c.

16   SCIENTIFIC CATALOGUE.

Macmillan (Rev. Hugh).—For other Works by the same Author, see THEOLOGICAL CATALOGUE.
HOLIDAYS ON HIGH LANDS; or, Rambles and Incidents in search of Alpine Plants. Globe 8vo. cloth. 6s.
FIRST FORMS OF VEGETATION. Second Edition, corrected and enlarged, with Coloured Frontispiece and numerous Illustrations. Globe 8vo. 6s.

Mansfield (C. B.).—Works by the late C. B. MANSFIELD :—
A THEORY OF SALTS. A Treatise on the Constitution of Bipolar (two-membered) Chemical Compounds. Crown 8vo. 14s.
AËRIAL NAVIGATION. The Problem, with Hints for its Solution. Edited by R. B. MANSFIELD. With a Preface by J. M. LUDLOW. With Illustrations. Crown 8vo. 10s. 6d.

Mayer.—SOUND : a Series of Simple, Entertaining, and Inexpensive Experiments in the Phenomena of Sound, for the Use of Students of every age. By A. M. MAYER, Professor of Physics in the Stevens Institute of Technology, &c. With numerous Illustrations. Crown 8vo. 3s. 6d. [*Nature Series.*

Mayer and Barnard.—LIGHT. A Series of Simple, Entertaining, and Useful Experiments in the Phenomena of Light, for the use of Students of every age. By A. M. MAYER and C. BARNARD. With Illustrations. Crown 8vo. 2s. 6d. [*Nature Series.*

Miall.—STUDIES IN COMPARATIVE ANATOMY. No. 1, The Skull of the Crocodile. A Manual for Students. By L. C. MIALL, Professor of Biology in Yorkshire College. 8vo. 2s. 6d. No. 2, The Anatomy of the Indian Elephant. By L. C. MIALL and F. GREENWOOD. With Plates. 5s.

Miller.—THE ROMANCE OF ASTRONOMY. By R. KALLEY MILLER, M.A., Fellow and Assistant Tutor of St. Peter's College, Cambridge. Second Edition, revised and enlarged. Crown 8vo. 4s. 6d.

Mivart (St. George).—Works by ST. GEORGE MIVART, F.R.S. &c., Lecturer in Comparative Anatomy at St. Mary's Hospital:—
ON THE GENESIS OF SPECIES. Second Edition, to which notes have been added in reference and reply to Darwin's "Descent of Man." With numerous Illustrations. Crown 8vo. 9s.
"*In no work in the English language has this great controversy been treated at once with the same broad and vigorous grasp of facts, and the same liberal and candid temper.*"—Saturday Review.

Mivart (St. George)—*continued.*
THE COMMON FROG. With Numerous Illustrations. Crown 8vo. 3s. 6d. (Nature Series.)

"*It is an able monogram of the Frog, and something more. It throws valuable crosslights over wide portions of animated nature. Would that such works were more plentiful.*"—Quarterly Journal of Science.

Moseley.—NOTES BY A NATURALIST ON THE "CHALLENGER," being an account of various observations made during the voyage of H.M.S. "Challenger" round the world in the years 1872—76. By H. N. MOSELEY, M.A.. F.R.S., Member of the Scientific Staff of the "Challenger." With Map, Coloured Plates, and Woodcuts. 8vo. 21s.

"*This is certainly the most interesting and suggestive book, descriptive of a naturalist's travels, which has been published since Mr. Darwin's 'Journal of Researches' appeared, now more than forty years ago. That it is worthy to be placed alongside that delightful record of the impressions, speculations, and reflections of a master mind, is, we do not doubt, the highest praise which Mr. Moseley would desire for his book, and we do not hesitate to say that such praise is its desert.*"—Nature.

Muir.—PRACTICAL CHEMISTRY FOR MEDICAL STUDENTS. Specially arranged for the first M. B. Course. By M. M. PATTISON MUIR, F.R.S.E. Fcap. 8vo. 1s. 6d.

Murphy.—HABIT AND INTELLIGENCE: a Series of Essays on the Laws of Life and Mind. By JOSEPH JOHN MURPHY. Second Edition, thoroughly revised and mostly rewritten. With Illustrations. 8vo. 16s.

Nature.—A WEEKLY ILLUSTRATED JOURNAL OF SCIENCE. Published every Thursday. Price 6d. Monthly Parts, 2s. and 2s. 6d. ; Half-yearly Volumes, 15s. Cases for binding Vols. 1s. 6d.

"*This able and well-edited Journal, which posts up the science of the day promptly, and promises to be of signal service to students and savants. . . . . Scarcely any expressions that we can employ would exaggerate our sense of the moral and theological value of the work.*"—British Quarterly Review.

Newcomb.—POPULAR ASTRONOMY. By SIMON NEWCOMB, LL.D., Professor U.S. Naval Observatory. With 112 Engravings and Five Maps of the Stars. 8vo. 18s.

"*As affording a thoroughly reliable foundation for more advanced reading, Professor Newcomb's 'Popular Astronomy' is deserving of strong recommendation.*"—Nature.

Oliver.—Works by DANIEL OLIVER, F.R.S., F.L.S., Professor of Botany in University College, London, and Keeper of the Herbarium and Library of the Royal Gardens, Kew :—

B

Oliver—*continued.*
LESSONS IN ELEMENTARY BOTANY. With nearly Two Hundred Illustrations. New Edition. Fcap. 8vo. 4s. 6d.
FIRST BOOK OF INDIAN BOTANY. With numerous Illustrations. Extra fcap. 8vo. 6s. 6d.
"*It contains a well-digested summary of all essential knowledge pertaining to Indian Botany, wrought out in accordance with the best principles of scientific arrangement.*"—Allen's Indian Mail.

Pasteur.—STUDIES ON FERMENTATION. The Diseases of Beer; their Causes and Means of Preventing them. By L. PASTEUR. A Translation of "Etudes sur la Bière," With Notes, Illustrations, &c. By F. FAULKNER & D. C. ROBB, B.A. 8vo. 21s.

Pennington.—NOTES ON THE BARROWS AND BONE CAVES OF DERBYSHIRE. With an account of a Descent into Elden Hole. By ROOKE PENNINGTON, B.A., LL.B., F.G.S. 8vo. 6s.

Penrose (F. C.)—ON A METHOD OF PREDICTING BY GRAPHICAL CONSTRUCTION, OCCULTATIONS OF STARS BY THE MOON, AND SOLAR ECLIPSES FOR ANY GIVEN PLACE. Together with more rigorous methods for the Accurate Calculation of Longitude. By F. C. PENROSE, F.R.A.S. With Charts, Tables, &c. 4to. 12s.

Perry.—AN ELEMENTARY TREATISE ON STEAM. By JOHN PERRY, B.E., Whitworth Scholar; Fellow of the Chemical Society, Lecturer in Physics at Clifton College. With numerous Woodcuts, Numerical Examples, and Exercises. New Edition. 18mo. 4s. 6d.
"*Mr. Perry has in this compact little volume brought together an immense amount of information, new told, regarding steam and its application, not the least of its merits being that it is suited to the capacities alike of the tyro in engineering science or the better grade of artisan.*"—Iron.

Pickering.—ELEMENTS OF PHYSICAL MANIPULATION. By E. C. PICKERING, Thayer Professor of Physics in the Massachusetts Institute of Technology. Part I., medium 8vo. 10s. 6d. Part II., 10s. 6d.
"*When finished 'Physical Manipulation' will no doubt be considered the best and most complete text-book on the subject of which it treats.*"—Nature.

Prestwich.—THE PAST AND FUTURE OF GEOLOGY. An Inaugural Lecture, by J. PRESTWICH, M.A., F.R.S., &c.: Professor of Geology, Oxford. 8vo. 2s.

Radcliffe.—PROTEUS: OR UNITY IN NATURE. By C. B. RADCLIFFE, M.D., Author of "Vital Motion as a mode of Physical Motion. Second Edition. 8vo. 7s. 6d.

Rendu.—THE THEORY OF THE GLACIERS OF SAVOY. By M. LE CHANOINE RENDU. Translated by A. WELLS, Q.C., late President of the Alpine Club. To which are added, the Original Memoir and Supplementary Articles by Professors TAIT and RUSKIN. Edited with Introductory remarks by GEORGE FORBES, B.A., Professor of Natural Philosophy in the Andersonian University, Glasgow. 8vo. 7s. 6d.

Roscoe.—Works by HENRY E. ROSCOE, F.R.S., Professor of Chemistry in the Victoria University, the Owens College, Manchester :—

LESSONS IN ELEMENTARY CHEMISTRY, INORGANIC AND ORGANIC. With numerous Illustrations and Chromolitho of the Solar Spectrum, and of the Alkalis and Alkaline Earths. New Edition. Fcap. 8vo. 4s. 6d.

CHEMICAL PROBLEMS, adapted to the above by Professor THORPE. Fifth Edition, with Key. 2s.

"*We unhesitatingly pronounce it the best of all our elementary treatises on Chemistry.*"—Medical Times.

PRIMER OF CHEMISTRY. Illustrated. 18mo. 1s.

Roscoe and Schorlemmer.—A TREATISE ON CHEMISTRY. With numerous Illustrations. By PROFESSORS ROSCOE and SCHORLEMMER. Vols. I. and II. Inorganic Chemistry.

Vol. I., The Non-metallic Elements. 8vo. 21s

Vol. II., Part I. Metals. 8vo. 18s.

Vol. II., Part II. Metals. 8vo. 18s.

Vol. III., Part I. Organic Chemistry. [*Immediately.*

"*Regarded as a treatise on the Non-metallic Elements, there can be no doubt that this volume is incomparably the most satisfactory one of which we are in possession.*"—Spectator.

"*It would be difficult to praise the work too highly. All the merits which we noticed in the first volume are conspicuous in the second. The arrangement is clear and scientific; the facts gained by modern research are fairly represented and judiciously selected; and the style throughout is singularly lucid.*"—Lancet.

Rumford (Count).—THE LIFE AND COMPLETE WORKS OF BENJAMIN THOMPSON, COUNT RUMFORD. With Notices of his Daughter. By GEORGE ELLIS. With Portrait, Five Vols. 8vo. 4l. 14s. 6d.

Schorlemmer.—A MANUAL OF THE CHEMISTRY OF THE CARBON COMPOUNDS OR ORGANIC CHEMISTRY. By C. SCHORLEMMER, F.R.S., Professor of Chemistry in the Victoria University, the Owens College, Manchester. 8vo. 14s.
"*It appears to us to be as complete a manual of the metamorphoses of carbon as could be at present produced, and it must prove eminently useful to the chemical student.*"—Athenæum.

Shann.—AN ELEMENTARY TREATISE ON HEAT, IN RELATION TO STEAM AND THE STEAM ENGINE. By G. SHANN, M.A. With Illustrations. Crown 8vo. 4s. 6d.

Smith.—HISTORIA FILICUM : An Exposition of the Nature, Number, and Organography of Ferns, and Review of the Principles upon which Genera are founded, and the Systems of Classification of the principal Authors, with a new General Arrangement, &c. By J. SMITH. A. L.S., ex-Curator of the Royal Botanic Garden, Kew. With Thirty Lithographic Plates by W. H. FITCH, F.L.S. Crown 8vo. 12s. 6d.
"*No one anxious to work up a thorough knowledge of ferns can afford to do without it.*"—Gardener's Chronicle.

South Kensington Science Lectures.
Vol. I.—Containing Lectures by Captain ABNEY, F.RS., Professor STOKES, Professor KENNEDY, F. J. BRAMWELL, F.R.S., Professor G. FORBES, H. C. SORBY, F.R.S., J. T. BOTTOMLEY, F.R.S.E., S. H. VINES, D.Sc., and Professor CAREY FOSTER. Crown 8vo. 6s.
Vol. II.—Containing Lectures by W. SPOTTISWOODE, P.R.S., Prof. FORBES, H. W. CHISHOLM, Prof. T. F. PIGOT, W. FROUDE, F.R.S., Dr. SIEMENS, Prof. BARRETT, Dr. BURDEN-SANDERSON, Dr. LAUDER BRUNTON, F.R.S., Prof. MCLEOD, Prof. ROSCOE, F.R.S., &c. Crown 8vo. 6s.

Spottiswoode.—POLARIZATION OF LIGHT. By W. SPOTTISWOODE, President of the Royal Society. With numerous Illustrations. Third Edition. Cr. 8vo. 3s. 6d. (Nature Series.)
"*The illustrations are exceedingly well adapted to assist in making the text comprehensible.*"—Athenæum. "*A clear, trustworthy manual.*"—Standard.

Stewart (B.).—Works by BALFOUR STEWART, F.R.S., Professor of Natural Philosophy in the Victoria University, the Owens College, Manchester:—
LESSONS IN ELEMENTARY PHYSICS. With numerous Illustrations and Chromolithos of the Spectra of the Sun, Stars, and Nebulæ. New Edition. Fcap. 8vo. 4s. 6d.
The Educational Times *calls this the beau-ideal of a scientific textbook, clear, accurate, and thorough.*"
PRIMER OF PHYSICS. With Illustrations. New Edition, with Questions. 18mo. 1s.

Stewart and Tait.—THE UNSEEN UNIVERSE; or, Physical Speculations on a Future State. By BALFOUR STEWART, F.R.S., and P. G. TAIT, M.A. Sixth Edition. Crown 8vo. 6s.

" *The book is one which well deserves the attention of thoughtful and religious readers. . . . It is a perfectly sober inquiry, on scientific grounds, into the possibilities of a future existence.*"—Guardian.

Stone.—ELEMENTARY LESSONS ON SOUND. By Dr. W. H. STONE, Lecturer on Physics at St. Thomas' Hospital. With Illustrations. Fcap. 8vo. 3s. 6d.

Tait.—LECTURES ON SOME RECENT ADVANCES IN PHYSICAL SCIENCE. By P. G. TAIT, M.A., Professor of Philosophy in the University of Edinburgh. Second edition, revised and enlarged, with the Lecture on Force delivered before the British Association. Crown 8vo. 9s.

Tanner.—Works by HENRY TANNER, F.C.S., Professor of Agricultural Science, University College, Aberystwith, Examiner in the Principles of Agriculture under the Government Department of Science.

FIRST PRINCIPLES OF AGRICULTURE. 18mo. 1s.

THE ABBOTT'S FARM; OR PRACTICE WITH SCIENCE. Crown 8vo. 3s. 6d.

THE ALPHABET OF THE PRINCIPLES OF AGRICULTURE, being a First Lesson Book in Agriculture for Schools. Extra fcap. 8vo. 6d.

FURTHER STEPS IN THE PRINCIPLES OF AGRICULTURE. [*In the press.*

Taylor.—SOUND AND MUSIC: A Non-Mathematical Treatise on the Physical Constitution of Musical Sounds and Harmony, including the Chief Acoustical Discoveries of Professor Helmholtz. By SEDLEY TAYLOR, M.A., late Fellow of Trinity College, Cambridge. Large crown 8vo. 8s. 6d.

"*In no previous scientific treatise do we remember so exhaustive and so richly illustrated a description of forms of vibration and of wave-motion in fluids.*"—Musical Standard.

Thomson.—Works by SIR WYVILLE THOMSON, K.C.B., F.R.S.

THE DEPTHS OF THE SEA: An Account of the General Results of the Dredging Cruises of H.M.SS. "Porcupine" and "Lightning" during the Summers of 1868-69 and 70, under the scientific direction of Dr. Carpenter, F.R.S., J. Gwyn Jeffreys, F.R.S., and Sir Wyville Thomson, F.R.S. With nearly 100 Illustrations and 8 coloured Maps and Plans. Second Edition. Royal 8vo. cloth, gilt. 31s. 6d.

The Athenæum *says: " The book is full of interesting matter, and is written by a master of the art of popular exposition. It is excellently illustrated, both coloured maps and woodcuts possessing high merit."*

Thomson—*continued.*
THE VOYAGE OF THE "CHALLENGER."—THE ATLANTIC. A Preliminary account of the Exploring Voyages of H.M.S. "Challenger," during the year 1873 and the early part of 1876. With numerous Illustrations, Coloured Maps & Charts, & Portrait of the Author, engraved by C. H. JEENS. 2 Vols. Medium 8vo. 45*s.*

The Times says :—"The paper, printing, and especially the numerous illustrations, are of the highest quality. . . . We have rarely, if ever, seen more beautiful specimens of wood engraving than abound in this work. . . . Sir Wyville Thomson's style is particularly attractive; he is easy and graceful, but vigorous and exceedingly happy in the choice of language, and throughout the work there are touches which show that science has not banished sentiment from his bosom."

Thudichum and Dupré.—A TREATISE ON THE ORIGIN, NATURE, AND VARIETIES OF WINE. Being a Complete Manual of Viticulture and Œnology. By J. L. W. THUDICHUM, M.D., and AUGUST DUPRÉ, Ph.D., Lecturer on Chemistry at Westminster Hospital. Medium 8vo. cloth gilt. 25*s.*

"A treatise almost unique for its usefulness either to the wine-grower, the vendor, or the consumer of wine. The analyses of wine are the most complete we have yet seen, exhibiting at a glance the constituent principles of nearly all the wines known in this country." —Wine Trade Review.

Tylor.—ANTHROPOLOGY: an Introduction to the Study of Man and Civilization. By E. B. TYLOR, D.C.L., F.R.S. With numerous Illustrations. Crown 8vo. 7*s.* 6*d.*

"If all manuals were like this, a generation over educated for its intellect would have no reason to complain. . . . A most attractive and entertaining introduction to the science of anthropology. . . . His writing is clear and luminous, and his arrangements masterly. . . . Mr. Tylor writes with as much caution as learning."— Saturday Review.

Wallace (A. R.).—Works by ALFRED RUSSEL WALLACE.
CONTRIBUTIONS TO THE THEORY OF NATURAL SELECTION. A Series of Essays. New Edition, with Corrections and Additions. Crown 8vo. 8*s.* 6*d.*

THE GEOGRAPHICAL DISTRIBUTION OF ANIMALS, with a study of the Relations of Living and Extinct Faunas as Elucidating the Past Changes of the Earth's Surface. With Maps, and numerous Illustrations by Zwecker. 2 vols. 8vo. 42*s.*

Wallace (A. R.)—*continued.*

The Times *says:* "*Altogether it is a wonderful and fascinating story whatever objections may be taken to theories founded upon it. Mr. Wallace has not attempted to add to its interest by any adornments of style; he has given a simple and clear statement of intrinsically interesting facts, and what he considers to be legitimate inductions from them. Naturalists ought to be grateful to him for having undertaken so toilsome a task. The work, indeed, is a credit to al concerned—the author, the publishers, the artist—unfortunately now no more—of the attractive illustrations—last but by no means least, Mr. Stanford's map-designer.*"

ISLAND LIFE; OR, THE PHENOMENA AND CAUSES OF INSULAR FAUNAS AND FLORAS, including a revision and attempted solution of the problem of geological climates. With Maps. 8vo. 18s.

"*Island Life is a work to be accepted almost without reservation from beginning to end . . . Whoever reads his book must be charmed with it.*"—St. James's Gazette. "*The work throughout abounds with interest . . . It may be read with equal pleasure by those who are already acquainted with the general principles of distribution and by those who wish for the first time to learn something about modern biological geography.*"—Athenæum "*The result of his work he has already given us in more th n one form; and his new volume on Island Life cont ins his latest views on the subject set forth in a clear and popular manner which should make them accessible to many readers who would not venture on the persual of his more strictly scientific expositions . . . Mr. Wallace has written nothing more clear, more masterly, or more convincing than this delightful volume.*"—Fortnightly Review.

TROPICAL NATURE: with other Essays. 8vo. 12s.

"*Nowhere amid the many descriptions of the tropics that have been given is to be found a summary of the past history and actual phenomena of the tropics which gives that which is distinctive of the phases of nature in them more clearly, shortly, and impressively.*"—Saturday Review.

Warington.—THE WEEK OF CREATION; OR, THE COSMOGONY OF GENESIS CONSIDERED IN ITS RELATION TO MODERN SCIENCE. By GEORGE WARINGTON, Author of "The Historic Character of the Pentateuch Vindicated." Crown 8vo. 4s. 6d.

Wilson.—RELIGIO CHEMICI. By the late GEORGE WILSON, M.D., F.R.S.E., Regius Professor of Technology in the University of Edinburgh. With a Vignette beautifully engraved after a design by Sir NOEL PATON. Crown 8vo. 8s. 6d.

Wilson (Daniel).—CALIBAN: a Critique on Shakespeare's "Tempest" and "Midsummer Night's Dream." By DANIEL WILSON, LL.D., Professor of History and English Literature in University College, Toronto. 8vo. 10s. 6d.

"*The whole volume is most rich in the eloquence of thought and imagination as well as of words. It is a choice contribution at once to science, theology, religion, and literature.*"—British Quarterly Review.

Wright.—METALS AND THEIR CHIEF INDUSTRIAL APPLICATIONS. By C. ALDER WRIGHT, D.Sc., &c., Lecturer on Chemistry in St. Mary's Hospital School. Extra fcap. 8vo. 3s. 6d.

Wurtz.—A HISTORY OF CHEMICAL THEORY, from the Age of Lavoisier down to the present time. By AD. WURTZ. Translated by HENRY WATTS, F.R.S. Crown 8vo. 6s.

"*The discourse, as a résumé of chemical theory and research, unites singular luminousness and grasp. A few judicious notes are added by the translator.*"—Pall Mall Gazette. "*The treatment of the subject is admirable, and the translator has evidently done his duty most efficiently.*"—Westminster Review.

SCIENCE PRIMERS FOR ELEMENTARY SCHOOLS.

Under the joint Editorship of Professors HUXLEY, ROSCOE, and BALFOUR STEWART.

Introductory. By Professor HUXLEY, F.R.S. 18mo. 1s.

Chemistry.—By H. E. ROSCOE, F.R.S., Professor of Chemistry in the Victoria University, the Owens College, Manchester. With numerous Illustrations. 18mo. 1s. New Edition. With Questions.

Physics.— By BALFOUR STEWART, F.R.S., Professor of Natural Philosophy in the Victoria University, the Owens College, Manchester. With numerous Illustrations. 18mo. 1s. New Edition. With Questions.

Physical Geography. — By ARCHIBALD GEIKIE, F.R.S., Murchison Professor of Geology and Mineralogy at Edinburgh. With numerous Illustrations. New Edition with Questions. 18mo. 1s.

Geology.—By Professor GEIKIE, F.R.S. With numerous Illustrations. New Edition. 18mo. cloth. 1s.

SCIENCE CLASS-BOOKS.

Science Primers for Elementary Schools—*continued.*

Physiology.—By MICHAEL FOSTER, M.D., F.R.S. With numerous Illustrations. New Edition. 18mo. 1s.

Astronomy.—By J. NORMAN LOCKYER, F.R.S. With numerous Illustrations. New Edition. 18mo. 1s.

Botany.—By Sir J. D. HOOKER, K.C.S.I., C.B., F.R.S. With numerous Illustrations. New Edition. 18mo. 1s.

Logic.—By STANLEY JEVONS, LL.D., M.A., F.R.S. New Edition. 18mo. 1s.

Political Economy.—By STANLEY JEVONS, LL.D., M.A., F.R.S. 18mo. 1s.

Others in preparation.

ELEMENTARY SCIENCE CLASS-BOOKS.

Agriculture.—ELEMENTARY LESSONS IN AGRICULTURAL SCIENCE. By H. TANNER, F.C.S., Professor of Agricultural Science, University College, Aberystwith.

[*Immediately.*

Astronomy.—By the ASTRONOMER ROYAL. POPULAR ASTRONOMY. With Illustrations. By Sir G. B. AIRY, K.C.B., Astronomer Royal. New Edition. 18mo. 4s. 6d.

Astronomy.—ELEMENTARY LESSONS IN ASTRONOMY. With Coloured Diagram of the Spectra of the Sun, Stars, and Nebulæ, and numerous Illustrations. By J. NORMAN LOCKYER, F.R.S. New Edition. Fcap. 8vo. 5s. 6d.

QUESTIONS ON LOCKYER'S ELEMENTARY LESSONS IN ASTRONOMY. For the Use of Schools. By JOHN FORBES ROBERTSON. 18mo, cloth limp. 1s. 6d.

Botany.—LESSONS IN ELEMENTARY BOTANY. By D. OLIVER, F.R.S., F.L.S., Professor of Botany in University College, London. With nearly Two Hundred Illustrations. New Edition. Fcap. 8vo. 4s. 6d.

Chemistry.—LESSONS IN ELEMENTARY CHEMISTRY, INORGANIC AND ORGANIC. By HENRY E. ROSCOE, F.R.S., Professor of Chemistry in the Victoria University, the Owens College, Manchester. With numerous Illustrations and Chromo-Litho of the Solar Spectrum, and of the Alkalies and Alkaline Earths. New Edition. Fcap. 8vo. 4s. 6d.

Elementary Science Class-books—*continued.*

A SERIES OF CHEMICAL PROBLEMS, prepared with Special Reference to the above, by T. E. THORPE, Ph.D., Professor of Chemistry in the Yorkshire College of Science, Leeds. Adapted for the preparation of Students for the Government, Science, and Society of Arts Examinations. With a Preface by Professor ROSCOE. New Edition, with Key. 18mo. 2*s.*

Practical Chemistry.—THE OWENS COLLEGE JUNIOR COURSE OF PRACTICAL CHEMISTRY. By FRANCIS JONES, F.R.S.E., F.C.S., Chemical Master in the Grammar School, Manchester. With Preface by Professor ROSCOE, and Illustrations. New Edition. 18mo. 2*s.* 6*d.*

Chemistry.—QUESTIONS ON. A Series of Problems and Exercises in Inorganic and Organic Chemistry. By F. JONES, F.R.S.E., F.C.S. 18mo. 3*s.*

Electricity and Magnetism.—By Professor SYLVANUS THOMPSON, of University College, Bristol. With Illustrations.
[*Immediately.*

Physiology.—LESSONS IN ELEMENTARY PHYSIOLOGY. With numerous Illustrations. By T. H. HUXLEY, F.R.S., Professor of Natural History in the Royal School of Mines. New Edition. Fcap. 8vo. 4*s.* 6*d.*

QUESTIONS ON HUXLEY'S PHYSIOLOGY FOR SCHOOLS. By T. ALCOCK, M.D. 18mo. 1*s.* 6*d.*

Political Economy.—POLITICAL ECONOMY FOR BEGINNERS. By MILLICENT G. FAWCETT. New Edition. 18mo. 2*s.* 6*d.*

Logic.—ELEMENTARY LESSONS IN LOGIC; Deductive and Inductive, with copious Questions and Examples, and a Vocabulary of Logical Terms. By W. STANLEY JEVONS, LLD., M.A., F.R.S. New Edition. Fcap. 8vo. 3*s.* 6*d.*

Physics.—LESSONS IN ELEMENTARY PHYSICS. By BALFOUR STEWART, F.R.S., Professor of Natural Philosophy in the Victoria University, the Owens College, Manchester. With numerous Illustrations and Chromo-Litho of the Spectra of the Sun, Stars, and Nebulæ. New Edition. Fcap. 8vo. 4*s.* 6*d.*

QUESTIONS ON STEWART'S LESSONS IN ELEMENTARY PHYSICS. By Professor T. H. CORE. 12mo. 2*s.*

Anatomy.—LESSONS IN ELEMENTARY ANATOMY. By ST. GEORGE MIVART, F.R.S., Lecturer in Comparative Anatomy at St. Mary's Hospital. With upwards of 400 Illustrations. Fcap. 8vo. 6*s.* 6*d.*

SCIENCE CLASS BOOKS.

Elementary Science Class-books—*continued.*

Mechanics.—AN ELEMENTARY TREATISE. By A. B. W. KENNEDY, C.E., Professor of Applied Mechanics in University College, London. With Illustrations. [*In preparation.*

Steam.—AN ELEMENTARY TREATISE. By JOHN PERRY, B.E., Whitworth Scholar; Fellow of the Chemical Society, Lecturer in Physics at Clifton College. With numerous Woodcuts and Numerical Examples and Exercises. New Edition. 18mo. 4s. 6d.

Physical Geography.—ELEMENTARY LESSONS IN PHYSICAL GEOGRAPHY. By A. GEIKIE, F.R.S., Murchison Professor of Geology, &c., Edinburgh. With numerous Illustrations. Fcap. 8vo. 4s. 6d.
QUESTIONS ON THE SAME. 1s. 6d.

Psychology.—ELEMENTARY LESSONS IN PSYCHOLOGY. By G. CROOM ROBERTSON, Professor of Mental Philosophy, &c., University College, London. [*In preparation.*

Geography.—CLASS-BOOK OF GEOGRAPHY. By C. B. CLARKE, M.A., F.G.S. New Edition, with eighteen coloured Maps. Fcap. 8vo. 3s.

Moral Philosophy.—AN ELEMENTARY TREATISE. By Professor E. CAIRD, of Glasgow University. [*In preparation.*

Natural Philosophy.—NATURAL PHILOSOPHY FOR BEGINNERS. By I. TODHUNTER, M.A., F.R.S. Part I. The Properties of Solid and Fluid Bodies. 18mo. 3s. 6d. Part II. Sound, Light, and Heat. 18mo. 3s. 6d.

The Economics of Industry.—By A. MARSHALL, M.A., late Principal of University College, Bristol, and MARY P. MARSHALL, late Lecturer at Newnham Hall, Cambridge. Extra fcap. 8vo. 2s. 6d.

Sound.—AN ELEMENTARY TREATISE. By Dr. W. H. STONE. With Illustrations. 18mo. 3s. 6d.

Easy Lessons in Science.—Edited by Professor W. F. BARRETT.
I. HEAT. By C. A. MARTINEAU. Illustrated. Extra fcap. 8vo. 2s. 6d.
II. LIGHT. By MRS. W. AWDRY. Illustrated. Extra fcap. 8vo. 2s 6d
Others in Preparation.

MANUALS FOR STUDENTS.

Crown 8vo.

Cossa.—GUIDE TO THE STUDY OF POLITICAL ECONOMY. By DR. LUIGI COSSA, Professor of Political Economy in the University of Pavia. Translated from the Second Italian Edition. With a Preface by W. STANLEY JEVONS, F.R.S. Crown 8vo. 4s. 6d.

Dyer and Vines.—THE STRUCTURE OF PLANTS. By Professor THISELTON DYER, F.R.S., assisted by SYDNEY VINES, B.Sc., Fellow and Lecturer of Christ's College, Cambridge. With numerous Illustrations. [*In preparation.*

Fawcett.—A MANUAL OF POLITICAL ECONOMY. By Right Hon. Henry FAWCETT, M.P. New Edition, revised and enlarged. Crown 8vo. 12s.

Fleischer.—A SYSTEM OF VOLUMETRIC ANALYSIS. Translated, with Notes and Additions, from the second German Edition, by M. M. PATTISON MUIR, F.R.S.E. With Illustrations. Crown 8vo. 7s. 6d.

Flower (W. H.).—AN INTRODUCTION TO THE OSTEOLOGY OF THE MAMMALIA. Being the Substance of the Course of Lectures delivered at the Royal College of Surgeons of England in 1870. By Professor W. H. FLOWER, F.R.S., F.R.C.S. With numerous Illustrations. New Edition, enlarged. Crown 8vo. 10s. 6d.

Foster and Balfour.—THE ELEMENTS OF EMBRYOLOGY. By MICHAEL FOSTER, M.D., F.R.S., and F. M. BALFOUR, M.A. Part I. crown 8vo. 7s. 6d.

Foster and Langley.—A COURSE OF ELEMENTARY PRACTICAL PHYSIOLOGY. By MICHAEL FOSTER, M.D., F.R.S., and J. N. LANGLEY, B.A. Fourth Edition. Crown 8vo. 6s.

Hooker (Dr.)—THE STUDENT'S FLORA OF THE BRITISH ISLANDS. By Sir J. D. HOOKER, K.C.S.I., C.B., F.R.S., M.D., D.C.L. New Edition, revised. Globe 8vo. 10s. 6d.

Huxley.—PHYSIOGRAPHY. An Introduction to the Study of Nature. By Professor HUXLEY, F.R.S. With numerous Illustrations, and Coloured Plates. New and cheaper Edition. Crown 8vo. 6s.

Manuals for Students—*continued*.

Huxley and Martin.—A COURSE OF PRACTICAL INSTRUCTION IN ELEMENTARY BIOLOGY. By Professor HUXLEY, F.R.S., assisted by H. N. MARTIN, M.B., D.Sc. New Edition, revised. Crown 8vo. 6s.

Huxley and Parker.—ELEMENTARY BIOLOGY. PART II. By Professor HUXLEY, F.R.S., assisted by T. J. PARKER. With Illustrations. [*In preparation.*

Jevons.—MANUALS. By W. STANLEY JEVONS, LL.D., M.A., F.R.S. :—

THE PRINCIPLES OF SCIENCE. A Treatise on Logic and Scientific Method. New and Revised Edition. Crown 8vo. 12s. 6d.
STUDIES IN DEDUCTIVE LOGIC. A Manual for Students. Crown 8vo. 6s.

Kennedy.—MECHANICS OF MACHINERY. By A. B. W. KENNEDY, M. Inst. C.E., Professor of Engineering and Mechanical Technology in University College, London. With Illustrations. Crown 8vo. [*In the Press.*

Kiepert.—A MANUAL OF ANCIENT GEOGRAPHY. From the German of Dr. H. KIEPERT. Crown 8vo. 5s.

Oliver (Professor).—FIRST BOOK OF INDIAN BOTANY. By Professor DANIEL OLIVER, F.R.S., F.L.S., Keeper of the Herbarium and Library of the Royal Gardens, Kew. With numerous Illustrations. Extra fcap. 8vo. 6s. 6d.

Parker and Bettany.—THE MORPHOLOGY OF THE SKULL. By Professor PARKER and G. T. BETTANY. Illustrated. Crown 8vo. 10s. 6d.

Tait.—AN ELEMENTARY TREATISE ON HEAT. By Professor TAIT, F.R.S.E. Illustrated. [*In the Press.*

Thomson.—ZOOLOGY. By Sir C. WYVILLE THOMSON, F.R.S. Illustrated. [*In preparation.*

Tylor—ANTHROPOLOGY: An Introduction to the Study of Man and Civilization. By E. B. TYLOR, M.A., F.R.S. Illustrated. Crown 8vo. 7s. 6d.

Other volumes of these Manuals will follow.

SCIENTIFIC TEXT-BOOKS.

Balfour.—A TREATISE ON COMPARATIVE EMBRYOLOGY. With Illustrations. By F. M. BALFOUR. M.A., F.R.S., Fellow and Lecturer of Trinity College, Cambridge. In 2 vols. 8vo. Vol. I. 18s. Vol II. 21s.

Ball (R.S., A.M.)—EXPERIMENTAL MECHANICS. A Course of Lectures delivered at the Royal College of Science for Ireland. By R. S. BALL, A.M., Professor of Applied Mathematics and Mechanics in the Royal College of Science for Ireland. Royal 8vo. 10s. 6d.

Chalmers.—GRAPHICAL DETERMINATION OF FORCES IN ENGINEERING STRUCTURES. By JAMES B. CHALMERS, C.E. With Illustrations. 8vo. 24s.

Clausius.—MECHANICAL THEORY OF HEAT. By R. CLAUSIUS. Translated by WALTER R. BROWNE, M.A., late Fellow of Trinity College, Cambridge. Crown 8vo. 10s. 6d.

Cotterill.—A TREATISE ON APPLIED MECHANICS. By JAMES COTTERILL, M.A., F.R.S., Professor of Applied Mechanics at the Royal Naval College, Greenwich. With Illustrations. 8vo. [*In preparation.*

Daniell.—A TREATISE ON PHYSICS FOR MEDICAL STUDENTS. By ALFRED DANIELL. With Illustrations. 8vo. [*In preparation.*

Foster.—A TEXT-BOOK OF PHYSIOLOGY. By MICHAEL FOSTER, M.D., F.R.S. With Illustrations. Third Edition, revised. 8vo. 21s.

Gamgee.—A TEXT-BOOK OF THE PHYSIOLOGICAL CHEMISTRY OF THE ANIMAL BODY. Including an account of the chemical changes occurring in Disease. By A. GAMGEE, M.D., F.R.S., Professor of Physiology in the Victoria University, the Owens College, Manchester. 2 vols. 8vo. With Illustrations. Vol. I. 18s. [*Vol. II. in the Press.*

Gegenbaur.—ELEMENTS OF COMPARATIVE ANATOMY. By Professor CARL GEGENBAUR. A Translation by F. JEFFREY BELL, B.A. Revised with Preface by Professor E. RAY LANKESTER, F.R.S. With numerous Illustrations. 8vo. 21s.

SCIENTIFIC TEXT-BOOKS. 31

Scientific Text-Books—*continued.*

Geikie.—TEXT-BOOK OF GEOLOGY. By ARCHIBALD GEIKIE, F.R.S., Professor of Geology in the University of Edinburgh. With numerous Illustrations. 8vo. [*Immediately.*

Gray.—STRUCTURAL BOTANY, OR, ORGANOGRAPHY ON THE BASIS OF MORPHOLOGY. To which are added the principles of Taxonomy and Phytography, and a Glossary of Botanical Terms. By Professor ASA GRAY, LL.D. 8vo. 10s. 6d.

Newcomb.—POPULAR ASTRONOMY. By S. NEWCOMB, LL.D., Professor U.S. Naval Observatory. With 112 Illustrations and 5 Maps of the Stars. 8vo. 18s.

"*It is unlike anything else of its kind, and will be of more use in circulating a knowledge of astronomy than nine-tenths of the books which have appeared on the subject of late years.*"—Saturday Review.

Reuleaux.—THE KINEMATICS OF MACHINERY. Outlines of a Theory of Machines. By Professor F. REULEAUX. Translated and Edited by Professor A. B. W. KENNEDY, C.E. With 450 Illustrations. Medium 8vo. 21s.

Roscoe and Schorlemmer.—INORGANIC CHEMISTRY. A Complete Treatise on Inorganic Chemistry. By Professor H. E. ROSCOE, F.R.S., and Professor C. SCHORLEMMER, F.R.S. With numerous Illustrations. Medium 8vo. Vol. I.—The Non-Metallic Elements. 21s. Vol. II.—Metals.—Part I. 18s. Vol. II.—Metals. Part II. 18s.

ORGANIC CHEMISTRY. A complete Treatise on Organic Chemistry. By Professors ROSCOE and SCHORLEMMER. With numerous Illustrations. Medium 8vo. Part I. [*Immediately.*

Schorlemmer.—A MANUAL OF THE CHEMISTRY OF THE CARBON COMPOUNDS, OR ORGANIC CHEMISTRY. By C. SCHORLEMMER, F.R.S., Professor of Chemistry, the Victoria University, the Owens College, Manchester. With Illustrations. 8vo. 14s.

Thorpe and Rücker.—A TREATISE ON CHEMICAL PHYSICS. By Professor THORPE, F.R.S., and Professor RÜCKER, of the Yorkshire College of Science. Illustrated. 8vo. [*In preparation.*

WORKS ON MENTAL AND MORAL PHILOSOPHY, AND ALLIED SUBJECTS.

Aristotle.—AN INTRODUCTION TO ARISTOTLE'S RHETORIC. With Analysis, Notes, and Appendices. By E. M. COPE, Trinity College, Cambridge. 8vo. 14s.

ARISTOTLE ON FALLACIES; OR, THE SOPHISTICI ELENCHI. With a Translation and Notes by EDWARD POSTE, M.A., Fellow of Oriel College, Oxford. 8vo. 8s. 6d.

ARISTOTLE.—The Metaphysics, Book I. Translated into English Prose, with Marginal Analysis, and Summary of each Chapter. By a Cambridge Graduate. Demy 8vo. 5s.

Balfour.—A DEFENCE OF PHILOSOPHIC DOUBT: being an Essay on the Foundations of Belief. By A. J. BALFOUR, M.P. 8vo. 12s.

"*Mr. Balfour's criticism is exceedingly brilliant and suggestive.*"—Pall Mall Gazette.

"*An able and refreshing contribution to one of the burning questions of the age, and deserves to make its mark in the fierce battle now raging between science and theology.*"—Athenæum.

Birks.—Works by the Rev. T. R. BIRKS, Professor of Moral Philosophy, Cambridge:—

FIRST PRINCIPLES OF MORAL SCIENCE; or, a First Course of Lectures delivered in the University of Cambridge. Crown 8vo. 8s. 6d.

This work treats of three topics all preliminary to the direct exposition of Moral Philosophy. These are the Certainty and Dignity of Moral Science, its Spiritual Geography, or relation to other main subjects of human thought, and its Formative Principles, or some elementary truths on which its whole development must depend.

MODERN UTILITARIANISM; or, The Systems of Paley, Bentham, and Mill, Examined and Compared. Crown 8vo. 6s. 6d.

SUPERNATURAL REVELATION; or, First Principles of Moral Theology. 8vo. 8s.

Boole.—AN INVESTIGATION OF THE LAWS OF THOUGHT, ON WHICH ARE FOUNDED THE MATHEMATICAL THEORIES OF LOGIC AND PROBABILITIES. By GEORGE BOOLE, LL.D., Professor of Mathematics in the Queen's University, Ireland, &c. 8vo. 14s.

Butler.—LECTURES ON THE HISTORY OF ANCIENT PHILOSOPHY. By W. ARCHER BUTLER, late Professor of Moral Philosophy in the University of Dublin. Edited from the Author's MSS., with Notes, by WILLIAM HEPWORTH THOMPSON, M.A., Master of Trinity College, and Regius Professor of Greek in the University of Cambridge. New and Cheaper Edition, revised by the Editor. 8vo. 12s.

Caird.—AN INTRODUCTION TO THE PHILOSOPHY OF RELIGION. By JOHN CAIRD, D.D., Principal and Vice-Chancellor of the University of Glasgow, and one of Her Majesty's Chaplains for Scotland. 8vo. 10s. 6d.

Caird.—A CRITICAL ACCOUNT OF THE PHILOSOPHY OF KANT. With an Historical Introduction. By E. CAIRD, M.A., Professor of Moral Philosophy in the University of Glasgow. 8vo. 18s.

Calderwood.—Works by the Rev. HENRY CALDERWOOD, M.A., LL.D., Professor of Moral Philosophy in the University of Edinburgh :—

PHILOSOPHY OF THE INFINITE: A Treatise on Man's Knowledge of the Infinite Being, in answer to Sir W. Hamilton and Dr. Mansel. Cheaper Edition. 8vo. 7s. 6d.

"*A book of great ability . . . . written in a clear stle, and may be easily understood by even those who are not versed in such discussions.*"—British Quarterly Review.

A HANDBOOK OF MORAL PHILOSOPHY. Sixth Edition. Crown 8vo. 6s.

"*A compact and useful work, going over a great deal of ground in a manner adapted to suggest and facilitate further study. . . . His book will be an assistance to many students outside his own University of Edinburgh.* —Guardian.

THE RELATIONS OF MIND AND BRAIN. 8vo. 12s.

" *Altogether his work is probably the best combination to be found at present in England of exposition and criticism on the subject of physiological psychology.*"—The Academy.

THE RELATIONS OF SCIENCE AND RELIGION. Being the Morse Lecturer, 1880, connected with Union Theological Seminary, New York. Crown 8vo. 5s.

Clifford.—LECTURES AND ESSAYS. By the late Professor W. K. CLIFFORD, F.R.S. Edited by LESLIE STEPHEN and FREDERICK POLLOCK, with Introduction by F. POLLOCK. Two Portraits. 2 vols. 8vo. 25s.

C

Clifford—*continued.*

"*The* Times *of October 22nd says:*—"*Many a friend of the author on first taking up these volumes and remembering his versatile genius and his keen enjoyment of all realms of intellectual activity must have trembled, lest they should be found to consist of fragmentary pieces of work, too disconnected to do justice to his powers of consecutive reading, and too varied to have any effect as a whole. Fortunately these fears are groundless. . . . It is not only in subject that the various papers are closely related. There is also a singular consistency of view and of method throughout. . . . It is in the social and metaphysical subjects that the richness of his intellect shows itself, most forcibly in the rarity and originality of the ideas which he presents to us. To appreciate this variety it is necessary to read the book itself, for it treats in some form or other of all the subjects of deepest interest in this age of questioning.*"

Fiske.—OUTLINES OF COSMIC PHILOSOPHY, BASED ON THE DOCTRINE OF EVOLUTION, WITH CRITICISMS ON THE POSITIVE PHILOSOPHY. By JOHN FISKE, M.A., LL.B., formerly Lecturer on Philosophy at Harvard University. 2 vols. 8vo. 25*s*.

"*The work constitutes a very effective encyclopædia of the evolutionary philosophy, and is well worth the study of all who wish to see at once the entire scope and purport of the scientific dogmatism of the day.*"—Saturday Review.

Harper.—THE METAPHYSICS OF THE SCHOOL. By the Rev. THOMAS HARPER (S.J.). In 5 vols. 8vo. Vol. I. 8vo. 18*s*. Vol. II. 8vo. 18*s*. [*Vol. III. in preparation.*

Herbert.—THE REALISTIC ASSUMPTIONS OF MODERN SCIENCE EXAMINED. By T. M. HERBERT, M.A., late Professor of Philosophy, &c., in the Lancashire Independent College, Manchester. 8vo. 14*s*.

"*Mr. Herbert's work appears to us one of real ability and importance. The author has shown himself well trained in philosophical literature, and possessed of high critical and speculative powers.*"—Mind.

Jardine.—THE ELEMENTS OF THE PSYCHOLOGY OF COGNITION. By ROBERT JARDINE, B.D., D.Sc., Principal of the General Assembly's College, Calcutta, and Fellow of the University of Calcutta. Crown 8vo. 6*s*. 6*d*.

Jevons.—Works by W. STANLEY JEVONS, LL.D., M.A., F.R.S.
THE PRINCIPLES OF SCIENCE. A Treatise on Logic and Scientific Method. New and Cheaper Edition, revised. Crown 8vo. 12s. 6d.
"*No one in future can be said to have any true knowledge of what has been done in the way of logical and scientific method in England without having carefully studied Professor Jevons' book.*"—Spectator.
THE SUBSTITUTION OF SIMILARS, the True Principle of Reasoning. Derived from a Modification of Aristotle's Dictum. Fcap. 8vo. 2s. 6d.
ELEMENTARY LESSONS IN LOGIC, DEDUCTIVE AND INDUCTIVE. With Questions, Examples, and Vocabulary of Logical Terms. New Edition. Fcap. 8vo. 3s. 6d.
STUDIES IN DEDUCTIVE LOGIC. A Manual for Students. Crown 8vo. 6s.
PRIMER OF LOGIC. New Edition. 18mo. 1s.

M'Cosh.—Works by JAMES M'COSH, LL.D., President of Princeton College, New Jersey, U.S.
"*He certainly shows himself skilful in that application of logic to psychology, in that inductive science of the human mind which is the fine side of English philosophy. His philosophy as a whole is worthy of attention.*"—Revue de Deux Mondes.
THE METHOD OF THE DIVINE GOVERNMENT, Physical and Moral. Tenth Edition. 8vo. 10s. 6d.
"*This work is distinguished from other similar ones by its being based upon a thorough study of physical science, and an accurate knowledge of its present condition, and by its entering in a deeper and more unfettered manner than its predecessors upon the discussion of the appropriate psychological, ethical, and theological questions. The author keeps aloof at once from the à priori idealism and dreaminess of German speculation since Scheling, and from the onesidedness and narrowness of the empiricism and positivism which have so prevailed in England.*"—Dr. Ulrici, in "Zeitschrift für Philosophie."

THE INTUITIONS OF THE MIND. A New Edition. 8vo. cloth. 10s. 6d.
"*The undertaking to adjust the claims of the sensational and intuitional philosophies, and of the à posteriori and à priori methods, is accomplished in this work with a great amount of success.*"—Westminster Review. "*I value it for its large acquaintance with English Philosophy, which has not led him to neglect the great German works. I admire the moderation and clearness, as well as comprehensiveness, of the author's views.*"—Dr. Dörner, of Berlin.

M'Cosh—*continued.*

AN EXAMINATION OF MR. J. S. MILL'S PHILOSOPHY: Being a Defence of Fundamental Truth. Second edition, with additions. 10s. 6d.

"*Such a work greatly needed to be done, and the author was the man to do it. This volume is important, not merely in reference to the views of Mr. Mill, but of the whole school of writers, past and present, British and Continental, he so ably represents.*"—Princeton Review.

THE LAWS OF DISCURSIVE THOUGHT: Being a Textbook of Formal Logic. Crown 8vo. 5s.

CHRISTIANITY AND POSITIVISM: A Series of Lectures to the Times on Natural Theology and Apologetics. Crown 8vo. 7s. 6d.

THE SCOTTISH PHILOSOPHY FROM HUTCHESON TO HAMILTON, Biographical, Critical, Expository. Royal 8vo. 16s.

THE EMOTIONS. Crown 8vo. 9s.

Masson.—RECENT BRITISH PHILOSOPHY: A Review

with Criticisms; including some Comments on Mr. Mill's Answer to Sir William Hamilton. By DAVID MASSON, M.A., Professor of Rhetoric and English Literature in the University of Edinburgh. Third Edition, with an Additional Chapter. Crown 8vo. 6s.

"*We can nowhere point to a work which gives so clear an exposition of the course of philosophical speculation in Britain during the past century, or which indicates so instructively the mutual influences of philosophic and scientific thought.*"—Fortnightly Review.

Materialism, Ancient and Modern. By a late Fellow

of Trinity College, Cambridge. Crown 8vo. 2s.

In this small volume the writer deals in six chapters with *Nature, Ancient Materialism, Modern Materialism, the Theory of Development, the Hypothesis of an Intelligent Cause,* and *the Hypothesis of Self-Existent Matter and Intelligence.*

Maudsley.—Works by H. MAUDSLEY, M.D., Professor of Medical

Jurisprudence in University College, London.

THE PHYSIOLOGY OF MIND; being the First Part of a Third Edition, Revised, Enlarged, and in great part Re-written, of "The Physiology and Pathology of Mind." Crown 8vo. 10s. 6d.

THE PATHOLOGY OF MIND. Revised, Enlarged, and in great part Re-written. 8vo. 18s.

BODY AND MIND: an Inquiry into their Connexion and Mutual Influence, specially with reference to Mental Disorders. An Enlarged and Revised edition. To which are added, Psychological Essays. Crown 8vo. 6s. 6d.

Maurice.—Works by the Rev. FREDERICK DENISON MAURICE, M.A., Professor of Moral Philosophy in the University of Cambridge. (For other Works by the same Author, see THEOLOGICAL CATALOGUE.)

SOCIAL MORALITY. Twenty-one Lectures delivered in the University of Cambridge. New and Cheaper Edition. Crown 8vo. 10s. 6d.

"*Whilst reading it we are charmed by the freedom from exclusiveness and prejudice, the large charity, the loftiness of thought, the eagerness to recognize and appreciate whatever there is of real worth extant in the world, which animates it from one end to the other. We gain new thoughts and new ways of viewing things, even more, perhaps, from being brought for a time under the influence of so noble and spiritual a mind.*"—Athenæum.

THE CONSCIENCE : Lectures on Casuistry, delivered in the University of Cambridge. New and Cheaper Edition. Crown 8vo. 5s.

The Saturday Review *says: "We rise from them with detestation of all that is selfish and mean, and with a living impression that there is such a thing as goodness after all.*"

MORAL AND METAPHYSICAL PHILOSOPHY. Vol. I. Ancient Philosophy from the First to the Thirteenth Centuries ; Vol. II. the Fourteenth Century and the French Revolution, with a glimpse into the Nineteenth Century. New Edition and Preface. 2 Vols. 8vo. 25s.

Morgan.—ANCIENT SOCIETY : or Researches in the Lines of Human Progress, from Savagery, through Barbarism to Civilisation. By LEWIS H. MORGAN, Member of the National Academy of Sciences. 8vo. 16s.

Murphy.—THE SCIENTIFIC BASES OF FAITH. By JOSEPH JOHN MURPHY, Author of "Habit and Intelligence." 8vo. 14s.

"*The book is not without substantial value; the writer continues the work of the best apologists of the last century, it may be with less force and clearness, but still with commendable persuasiveness and tact; and with an intelligent feeling for the changed conditions of the problem.*"—Academy.

Paradoxical Philosophy.—A Sequel to "The Unseen Universe." Crown 8vo. 7s. 6d.

Picton.—THE MYSTERY OF MATTER AND OTHER ESSAYS. By J. ALLANSON PICTON, Author of "New Theories and the Old Faith." Cheaper issue with New Preface. Crown 8vo. 6s.

Picton—*continued.*
CONTENTS :— *The Mystery of Matter—The Philosophy of Ignorance—The Antithesis of Faith and Sight—The Essential Nature of Religion—Christian Pantheism.*

Sidgwick.—THE METHODS OF ETHICS. By HENRY SIDGWICK, M.A., Prælector in Moral and Political Philosophy in Trinity College, Cambridge. Second Edition, revised throughout with important additions. 8vo. 14s.

A SUPPLEMENT to the First Edition, containing all the important additions and alterations in the Second. 8vo. 2s.

"*This excellent and very welcome volume. . . . . Leaving to metaphysicians any further discussion that may be needed respecting the already over-discussed problem of the origin of the moral faculty, he takes it for granted as readily as the geometrician takes space for granted, or the physicist the existence of matter. But he takes little else for granted, and defining ethics as 'the science of conduct,' be carefully examines, not the various ethical systems that have been propounded by Aristotle and Aristotle's followers downwards, but the principles upon which, so far as they confine themselves to the strict province of ethics, they are based.*"—Athenæum.

Thornton.—OLD-FASHIONED ETHICS, AND COMMON-SENSE METAPHYSICS, with some of their Applications. By WILLIAM THOMAS THORNTON, Author of "A Treatise on Labour." 8vo. 10s. 6d.

The present volume deals with problems which are agitating the minds of all thoughtful men. The following are the Contents:— I. Ante-Utilitarianism. II. History's Scientific Pretensions. III. David Hume as a Metaphysician. IV. Huxleyism. V. Recent Phase of Scientific Atheism. VI. Limits of Demonstrable Theism.

Thring (E., M.A.).—THOUGHTS ON LIFE-SCIENCE. By EDWARD THRING, M.A. (Benjamin Place), Head Master of Uppingham School. New Edition, enlarged and revised. Crown 8vo. 7s. 6d.

Venn.—Works by JOHN VENN, M.A., Fellow and Lecturer of Gonville and Caius College, Cambridge.

THE LOGIC OF CHANCE: An Essay on the Foundations and Province of the Theory of Probability, with especial reference to its logical bearings, and its application to Moral and Social Science. Second Edition, rewritten and greatly enlarged. Crown 8vo. 10s. 6d.

SYMBOLIC LOGIC. Crown 8vo. 10s. 6d.

Watson.—KANT AND HIS ENGLISH CRITICS. A Comparison of Critical and Empirical Philosophy. By JOHN WATSON, M.A., LL.D., Professor of Moral Philosophy in Queen's University, Kingston, Canada. 8vo. 12s. 6d.

NATURE SERIES.

THE SPECTROSCOPE AND ITS APPLICATIONS. By J. N. LOCKYER, F.R.S. With Illustrations. *Second Edition.* Crown 8vo. 3s. 6d.

THE ORIGIN AND METAMORPHOSES OF INSECTS. By Sir JOHN LUBBOCK, M.P., F.R.S. With Illustrations. *Second Edition.* Crown 8vo. 3s. 6d.

THE TRANSIT OF VENUS. By G. FORBES, B.A., Professor of Natural Philosophy in the Andersonian University, Glasgow. With numerous Illustrations. Crown 8vo. 3s. 6d.

THE COMMON FROG. By ST. GEORGE MIVART, F.R.S. Illustrated. Crown 8vo. 3s. 6d.

POLARISATION OF LIGHT. By W. SPOTTISWOODE, LL.D., President of the Royal Society. Illustrated. *Second Edition.* Crown 8vo. 3s. 6d.

ON BRITISH WILD FLOWERS CONSIDERED IN RELATION TO INSECTS. By SIR JOHN LUBBOCK, M.P., F.R.S. Illustrated. *Second Edition.* Crown 8vo. 4s. 6d.

THE SCIENCE OF WEIGHING AND MEASURING. By H. W. CHISHOLM, Warden of the Standards. Illustrated. Crown 8vo. 4s. 6d.

HOW TO DRAW A STRAIGHT LINE: A Lecture on Linkages. By A. B. KEMPE, B.A. Illustrated. Crown 8vo. 1s. 6d.

LIGHT: A Series of Simple, Entertaining and Useful Experiments in the Phenomena of Light for the Use of Students of every Age. By ALFRED M. MAYER and CHARLES BARNARD. With Illustrations. Crown 8vo. 2s. 6d.

SOUND: A Series of Simple, Entertaining and Inexpensive Experiments in the Phenomena of Sound, for the Use of Students of every Age. By A. M. MAYER, Professor of Physics in the Stevens Institute of Technology, &c. With numerous Illustrations. Crown 8vo. 3s. 6d.

SEEING AND THINKING. By Prof. W. K. CLIFFORD, F.R.S. With Diagrams. Crown 8vo. 3s. 6d.

DEGENERATION. A Chapter in Darwinism. By Professor E. RAY LANKESTER, F.R.S. Crown 8vo. 2s. 6d.

FASHION IN DEFORMITY, as Illustrated in the Customs of Barbarous and Civilized Races. By WILLIAM HENRY FLOWER, LL.D., F.R.S., &c. With Illustrations. Crown 8vo. 2s. 6d.

(*Other Volumes to follow.*)

MACMILLAN AND CO., LONDON.

Published every Thursday, price 6d.; Monthly Parts, 2s. and 2s. 6d., Half-Yearly Volumes, 15s.

NATURE:
AN ILLUSTRATED JOURNAL OF SCIENCE.

NATURE expounds in a popular and yet authentic manner, the GRAND RESULTS OF SCIENTIFIC RESEARCH, discussing the most recent scientific discoveries, and pointing out the bearing of Science upon civilisation and progress, and its claims to a more general recognition, as well as to a higher place in the educational system of the country.

It contains original articles on all subjects within the domain of Science; Reviews setting forth the nature and value of recent Scientific Works; Correspondence Columns, forming a medium of Scientific discussion and of intercommunication among the most distinguished men of Science, Serial Columns, giving the gist of the most important papers appearing in Scientific Journals, both Home and Foreign; Transactions of the principal Scientific Societies and Academies of the World, Notes, &c.

In Schools where Science is included in the regular course of studies, this paper will be most acceptable, as it tells what is doing in Science all over the world, is popular without lowering the standard of Science, and by it a vast amount of information is brought within a small compass, and students are directed to the best sources for what they need. The various questions connected with Science teaching in schools are also fully discussed, and the best methods of teaching are indicated.

LONDON: R. CLAY, SONS, AND TAYLOR, PRINTERS.

www.ingramcontent.com/pod-product-compliance
Lightning Source LLC
Chambersburg PA
CBHW030019240426
43672CB00007B/1015